I0161027

More Stories I Lived

*Buy this Book Please
I Need a New Car ...
My Old One Shrunk!*

Ken Campbell

TEACH Services, Inc.
PUBLISHING
www.TEACHServices.com • (800) 367-1844

Copyright © 2022 Ken Campbell
Copyright © 2022 TEACH Services, Inc.
ISBN-13: 978-1-4796-1485-1 (Paperback)
ISBN-13: 978-1-4796-1486-8 (ePub)
Library of Congress Control Number: 2022907598

All Scripture quotations are from the King James Version.

TEACH Services, Inc.
P U B L I S H I N G
www.TEACHServices.com • (800) 367-1844

About the Author

Ken Campbell was born in San Jose, California, and raised by Lemanasky Lake in Washington state. Known for his various roles as a rancher, mechanic, auto dealer, radio broadcast host, storyteller, and inspirational speaker, Campbell has a devoted following among his customers, family, friends, and young audience, which has grown as more people are getting to know him through his books, *Stories I Lived* and *More Stories I Lived*. Whenever he wants to write, he says, all he has to do is return to the mountains where he was raised, and the stories come tumbling back to mind. Reading his book, you will travel back with him as he reminisces about his childhood home and the lessons he learned. Campbell now lives in Deer Park, Washington.

Table of Contents

Preface

Perhaps, right at the outset, an explanation (or is it an apology?) is in order: Some people who have read my first book, *Stories I Lived*, have asked, "How long did it take you to write this book?" My usual honest answer is: "Most of my life!"

Many years ago, at the Christmas-New Year season, my wife, Eleanor, and I were sending out hundreds of individual greeting cards to relatives, friends, customers, and some listeners to my then "Christian Radio Broadcast." This was getting to be quite a hassle.

When Eleanor suggested that we should just send out a form letter to all of them, I, at first, balked at her "one size fits all" idea. But, in 1989, I relented and came up with the "wise" (ha!) idea of including a story from my (our) life with each form letter. Sort of a "bribe" or reward especially for those who know or care little about the more personal aspects of our lives or the lives of our relatives. *Sneaky, eh?*

In short, this almost accidentally began somewhat of a tradition. Kind (and probably flattering) people began to say how they always looked forward to next year's story and said, "Kenny, you should put them in a book." Thus, my first book, *Stories I Lived*, and now this one, *More Stories I Lived*, come to you wise and discerning readers somewhat by accident from a not very famous or complicated writer.

Hopefully, however, if you buy it and read it, you will decide that you're doing so was not an accident but that you needed that laugh or that inspiration.

With all this in mind, as you will see, I have left the dates in some of the stories, believing that the story is not and will not become outdated.

The first story, "Joyous Surprise," was written in 1989 and is the one which started all this. Unless you are badly mathematically challenged, you may also correctly calculate that I, the not very famous but appreciative author, am well into advanced "geezerhood" at this time.

BLESSINGS!

Thanks to my address being in the book, I get feedback now and then.

Kenny
P.O. Box 1715
Deer Park, WA 99006

1.

Joyous Surprise

Christmas morning and snow—lots of snow—like three to four feet on the level. Noisy crackling fires in both the kitchen and living room wood stoves exuded cheerful snugness and heat into the drafty little farmhouse squatting among the trees a hundred yards or so from Lemanasky Lake.

Good ol' Lemanasky Lake—Dad had already assured us that the ice on the lake was nearly three feet thick, and, yes, there would be plenty of it for making ice cream come the Fourth of July and the annual Pine Creek community picnic.

But for three energetic farm boys, winter and snow and ice without sleds were about as cheering as a visit to the candy store without any money. We had no sleds, and we most certainly had no money.

"First thing this morning, Stan, you and Kenny better go out and check on the calves in the old Didra barn—it's pretty cold outside today." Dad's wish was, for certain, our command. We laboriously struggled into our heavy, cumbersome cold weather outfits. Then, moving slowly, or, better said, ponderously, like two pint-sized moonwalkers (before there even were such "critters"), we wallowed our way out through the deep snow to the old log barn.

Laboriously we pushed the heavy door open and, at first, gasped with surprise and then shrieked with delight. It's been at least fifty long years since that day, but, in my mind's eye, "they" are still there, frozen in time, still gleaming and brand new. There they stand—three honest to goodness, genuine store-bought sleds! There was a large one for big brother Stan, a middle-sized one for me, and a short, stubby one for little brother Garry.

With "eager reluctance," I rouse myself from my reverie and try to accept the sobering fact that it is Christmas 1989! Just a few weeks ago, at dusk, I sat alone on the remote mountain west of Lemanasky Lake, right where I loved to sit alone some fifty years ago.

I ached with sadness and savored strange emptiness from the realization that the old Campbell place below is now only a broken down, crumbling basement and a few decaying scraps of lumber cut—no doubt—in Uncle Ed Hall's wondrous sawmill. I thanked God that I am old enough to have forgotten the hard bitter things of childhood yet still young enough to remember and appreciate the good things, past and present.

Dad is only a memory now and Mom, God bless her, no longer remembers Pine Creek, and Lemanasky Lake, or Tonasket, or Christmas, or, for that matter, even very much about us "kids." It somehow seems almost disrespectful that the ancient Didra log barn still stands. It was there long before the day Dad "hid" those three new sleds in it; it was there even prior to the arrival of our hardy cousins, the "Hall Kids." Is it perhaps mocking our mortality?

"Slower than molasses in January" is an expression I readily relate to, but, pray tell, what juvenile neophyte coined the ridiculous phrase, "slower than Christmas"? It seems to me that Christmas arrives sooner with each passing year!

This year has lifted us to the refreshing heights of happiness and contentment and, as well, plunged us down and into the swamplands of sorrow and disappointment. No doubt many of you can agree with this. We trust, however, that *you*, with us, can agree that life *is* very well *worth the living*.

2.

The Tin Boat

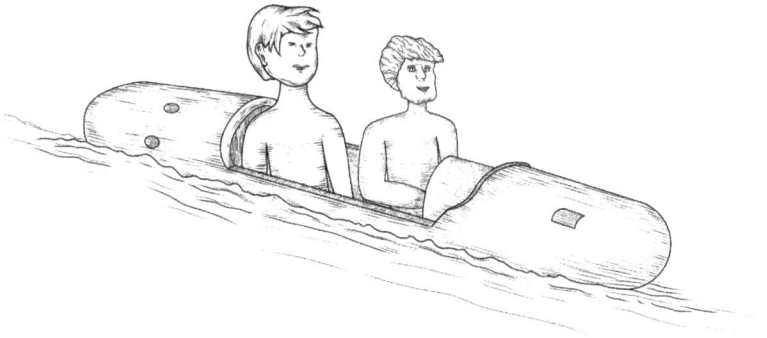

    If I close my eyes tightly and concentrate really hard, I can almost—but not quite—convince myself that I can still see the *Popular Mechanics* magazine advertisement which hooked me so many years ago. This much is certain, however, my memory of the advertised item is still perfectly clear … because I bought it. I did so in spite of the fact that, financially speaking, the investment pretty well wiped me out.

The ad accurately stated that it was half of a gas tank from a certain World War II airplane. (I've forgotten which type of airplane.) The ad touted it as being suitable as a planter, livestock watering trough, boat, etc. The word "boat" is the one that launched me into some delightful daydreaming and, as well, became the cause of vividly real, genuine night-time dreams. I was obsessed with the possibility of becoming the only thirteen-year-old kid in the county with his very own personal boat. Truly astounding!

When I excitedly showed the advertisement to Dad, he, of course, responded in predictable adult fashion, pointing out that such a "craft" would be extremely prone to tipping over, thus dunking its captain into the drink. I had a ready answer to this objection: "Yeah, Dad, but I can swim!" This glib answer was actually an extremely shallow one. I was (and am) a lousy swimmer—my best swimming "stroke" being most accurately described as a combination of dog paddling, frantic water treading, water gulping, and drowning. *But*—since this was also Dad's style of swimming, and since it was also one of the few things I could do as well or better than he—it somewhat trumped his argument. I, of course, also promised to "stay close to the shore," which was a safely subjective term.

Perhaps Dad also fell for my suggestion that, if it didn't pan out as a boat, we could always use it as a livestock trough. If I recall correctly, the price was on the order of $3.95, plus shipping and handling. I forked the huge amount over to Dad, and he wrote a check to the company. I joyously mailed the order for my "yacht," then my interminably lengthy waiting period began.

It seemed like forever, but at last came the glorious day when, instead of leaving the mail in our box out at the end of our lane, Vern, the faithful mail carrier, drove in and backed up near our front gate. I happened to be out at the barn, so I watched as he got out and walked around to the rear of his pickup. I cannot accurately convey the excitement I felt as I watched Vern pull a long, shiny, teardrop shaped bulky item out of the pickup box, then, with some difficulty, carefully balance it on end against one of the gate posts. My boat had arrived. I nearly stumbled over a cow in my haste to get out of the barn and take possession of it!

It was at least as large as I had expected, it was even shinier than I had dared to hope, and—*oh, no!*—the ad had forgotten to tell me that my metal boat had three large holes in it, holes which, no doubt, as filler, vent, or gauge holes, were required during its previous service as an airplane gas tank. I was heartsick and devastated. I could, perhaps, stuff a rag into the one-inch hole, but what could I possibly do with the approximately three- and four-inch ones? As Dad said, "Man! You could throw a cat through those holes!"

Dad saw how disappointed I was and, at first, tried to cheer me by saying, "Well, Kenny, maybe the holes could be welded shut," but then after a long pause he dolefully added, "But I'm afraid that would cost more than the d—n thing is worth." The dark cloud of gloom which enveloped me lifted slightly when Dad continued, "Well, Kenny, it won't cost anything to find out. The next time we go to town we can take it along to the machine shop, and *you* can find out."

Dad meant that *"you"* literally, and I now suppose that it was because he wanted me to learn how to take responsibility for my own actions. In any event, when we, at long last, went to the machine shop in Tonasket, Dad said, "It's your boat, Kenny. You can do the talking." This scared me, but desire spurred me on.

At my request, the machine shop man came out to the pickup and slowly, carefully studied the large holes. I studied his face and waited breathlessly. Finally, he said, "Yes, I can fix 'em. I can braze patches over them."

Now must come the simple question, the one I most feared to ask: "How much would that cost?" The big man shoved the funny looking welding goggles up higher on his forehead, then looked me straight in the eyes and asked with a grin, "Well, son, how much do you have?" I gulped and rather meekly replied, "A dollar and fifty cents." The machine shop man gave Dad a quick wink, which I did not understand until much later, and then chuckled and loudly declared on this wise: "Well, what do you know! That just happens to be exactly how much it will cost!"

Now, friends, bear with me as we wander down an important little side path for a brief moment. That machine shop man just "happened" to be a Christian, the late Mr. George Churchman.

Could it be that the simple little incident I've just related, one about which Mr. Churchman, in all likelihood, hardly gave a second thought, might have been one of the reasons my oftentimes bitter non-Christian Dad was "forced" to add *him* to the too short list of Christians with whom he could find little or no fault? I, of course, did not realize it at the time, but I am now quite certain the measly $1.50 he "charged" me did not cover even the cost of the materials, much less did it leave any for his labor. There's a lesson there for those of us who profess to be Christians.

Thus, my boat was fixed, and it didn't leak a drop. This was most comforting in view of the fact that I had to sit right down low directly on the bottom to keep it from tipping over. Even so, it still was so precarious that I paddled gingerly and took shallow breaths for fear of capsizing.

The tin boat was much too large and heavy and awkward to carry under an arm or in front of me. I didn't dare drag it for fear of damaging it—at least if the terrain to a lake was rugged and rocky, which it usually was. At that time, my little brother Garry was too small to carry one end, at least not very far. Thus, my usual method for transporting it was to heft it up on top of my head, where it smashed my cowboy hat down over my eyes and ears and gave me a stiff neck and a sore head as its sharp metal edges cut into the palms of my hands.

And it was no fun blindly ramming into trees, tripping over rocks, and struggling through clinging brush as I strove mightily to keep my bearings and stay on course in the general direction of the lake. At such trying times, the laughter bursting forth from my bothersome brother Garry, and my pesky little sister Sherry did little to cheer or encourage me along. Indeed, I found it quite exasperating. They, however, full well knew that, by the time I could carefully ease the cumbersome boat down off my head and push my hat back up so I could see them, they could be long gone. I would then have to rassle my awkward, imbalanced burden back up on top again. My strength was limited to but a few such strenuous ordeals, thus they knew they were perfectly safe enjoying my misery.

Dad loved to fish, although, at that time, he seldom took time off work at the ranch to do so. I well remember one time when we went all the way down to Fish Lake, and Dad let me take my boat. I don't think Dad had much fun fishing that day. He spent much of his time going up and down the bank of the lake watching me and hollering for me to come back in closer to the shore.

Looking back, I now fully understand why he was so worried. The tippy tin boat would have sunk like the proverbial rock, I was fully clothed, and I had no life jacket, indeed, had never even heard of such a thing. Which brings us to the primary point of my story—

It was a lovely spring day, and I had a severe case of spring fever. With little brother in tow, I lugged the tin boat a quarter mile or more up the hill and out through the sagebrush, rocks, and "dingles" to the School Section Lake. It seemed well worth the effort. I had a grand time paddling around, although I did feel a mite sorry for Garry just sitting there on the bank. Whenever I came anywhere near him he'd holler, "Let me ride in the boat!"

From what Dad and Mom had said, I was quite certain they would not approve of me letting him out in the boat alone. Moreover, I didn't want to risk losing it. So, at last I said, "OK, but you have to sit real still right here on the bottom between my legs." Garry sat so very still and was so happy. Things were going so nicely that, almost without being aware of it, we soon found ourselves a goodly distance from the shore of the small lake. Then it happened—

A mother duck came gliding out of the cattails and lily pads with a string of tiny, cute ducklings parading along in single file right behind her. "Looky there!" shouted Garry as he jerked around to point at them. In much less time than it takes to tell it, we were in the water. The next thing I knew, I found myself grasping my tin boat with one hand and little brother with the other. He was wide-eyed, frantically kicking and threshing and spouting water. I suspect I fit the same description. However, a perplexing thought was also flooding my mind: I could possibly

The next thing I knew, I found myself grasping my tin boat with one hand and little brother with the other.

save myself and the boat or myself and little brother, but I knew that I could not save both the boat and my brother! Which one would I let go of first?

Fortunately, I never had to make that decision. I'm fairly certain, or at least I certainly hope, that I would have hung onto little brother! In truth, however, he was hanging onto me so tightly I probably could not have shaken him off even if I had wanted to.

Then, all of a sudden, I felt a whole lot better. Quite unexpectedly I found myself standing on the bottom. Oh, to be sure it wasn't a very firm bottom, in fact it was soft and muddy, but it was, nonetheless holding me up. The water came only a little higher than half way up my chest.

It required some loud screaming, "Put your feet down! Put your feet down!" But the welcome message finally burst through Garry's wall of frantic fear, and he put his feet down. Then, laughing almost hysterically with relief, we wallowed our way out through the deep, slimy, yucky, *beautiful* mud to safety, dragging the tin boat in our wake.

I am reminded that the Blessed Book declares, "The just shall live by faith" (Hebrews 10:38; Habakkuk 2:4). The Bible also assures us that Jesus Christ is the *solid rock* of our salvation. But sometimes I'm too busy kicking as my last resort to put my feet down. How is it with you, friend?

One final, intriguing, puzzling thought comes to me just now since this is not a mere made-up "story." I actually lived the incidents I have related here, and they impressed me deeply. So, why is it then that I cannot—for the life of me—remember whatever became of my "precious" tin boat? Perhaps it is that my fondness for it was simply superseded by more interesting things, such as cars and girls!

"Delight thyself also in the LORD, and *he* shall give thee the [best and proper] desires of thine heart" (Ps. 37:4).

3.

Hunters, Knives, and Belated Gifts

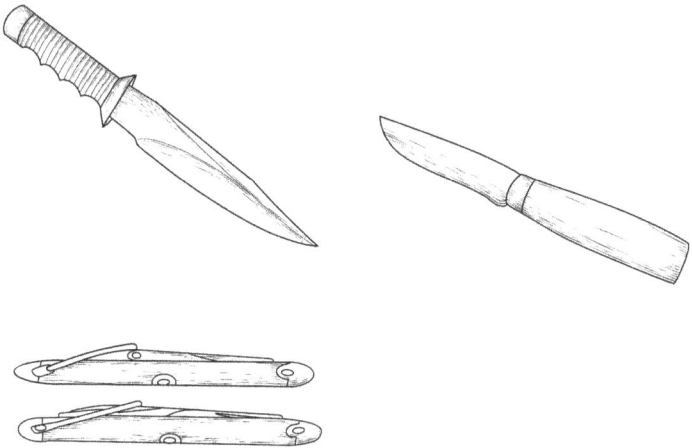

No doubt it was because our Pine Creek community was so remote, with neighbors few and far between. At any rate, we knew who owned nearly every truck, car, pickup, or saddle horse that, from time to time, chanced to travel up or down the primitive road that meandered by our house at Lemanasky Lake. There was, however, one time of the year that added an exciting and almost mysterious element to the usual, readily recognized sightings of passersby.

Late in the fall, for two or three weeks, we would closely scrutinize unfamiliar vehicles as they hurried by at rather "cityfied" speeds. Dad would observe, "It must be hunting season." This soon would be confirmed as the hills came alive with the sound of shooting. The crisp, sharp, usually single crack of a small-bore rifle was not uncommon. It simply informed us that some neighboring rancher or rancher's kid had swiftly, accurately, and probably painlessly harvested a few meals or dispensed with some marauding rodent or predator.

The sounds of what we termed "city dude hunting season" were much different. These were the deep, heavy BOOM! BOOM! BOOM! of large caliber rifles. Oftentimes we would count off as many as seven or eight shots with only a second or two between each BOOM. Dad would scoff, "That guy must be a lousy shot, and, if he isn't and he actually hit that poor deer with even half those bullets, the meat won't be fit to eat anyway!"

It may be different now, but in that time, place, and culture, the natives and especially the "old timers" tended to look down their noses at what they labeled "unsportsman-type city dudes" who relied upon long-range, rapid-fire shooting with semi-automatic, telescopic, high-power rifles. Real hunters, respectable sportsmen, they insisted, relied upon skillful, quiet, patient stalking, and accurate, close range, quick, clean kills.

I remember one occasion when my friend Billy and I were on horseback and came upon a small hunter lugging a huge rifle. He also toted a large pistol on each hip. Each revolver dangled clumsily from a wide cartridge belt completely encircled with short, fat bullets. On his torso he wore a red vest that had loops filled with the largest cartridges we curious country boys had ever seen. They looked like cannon shells to us!

When at last we could speak, having so suddenly and unexpectedly come upon such an awesome and fearful figure standing in the middle of the trail, Billy politely asked, "What caliber is that rifle, Mister?" The mighty city hunter proudly replied, "45.70." Billy kinda gasped, then spontaneously croaked, "Mister—there ain't no lions or elephants out here!"

The short city dude hunter mumbled something we didn't catch, then plodded heavily on down the trail, a big round canteen slapping him on the rump with each and every short, choppy step. It was most impressive.

For us, however, the best part of hunting season came when it was over, and all the hunters had packed up and gone home. Mind you, this was long before pickup campers and plush, comfortable, self-contained motorhomes. We're talking cold nights and tarps or tents, sleeping bags, and range cattle pastures complete with fresh cow "patties" here and there and everywhere. I guess such inhospitable camping facilities must have motivated the hunters to drink—at least most of them seemed to do a lot of it.

In those days of yore, before aluminum cans, came beer bottles. And with beer bottles—oh happy days!—came money. We got a penny for small brown bottles, and three whole, wonderful pennies for large ones. Once in a great while, we'd even find very special bottles, some of which could be traded in for the vast sum of a nickel—the total price of a genuine, store-bought ice cream cone!

We sometimes found other treasures as well, such as unfired cartridges, playing cards, coins, and, yes, even chewing tobacco and cigarettes, which I wish I could honestly say we always dutifully turned over to our daddies or promptly threw away. (On the other hand, however, perhaps it all worked out for the best in the long run, since I got so sick that I, then and there, swore off tobacco for life!)

But comes now the hunter's camp scouting incident that is burned deeply into my memory bank. I was concentrating on an area of an abandoned camp where trampled grass indicated a tent probably had stood. Billy was off at the perimeter combing the brush for bottles when he suddenly let out with a loud whoop of obvious joy. "Looky what I found!" he exulted, as he dashed toward me. He held up a hunting knife in what appeared to be a like-new leather sheath. When he pulled the knife out, it was sharp and shiny, in fact, it too was in like-new condition.

I was happy for friend Billy, but I must admit I was also a bit jealous, knowing that he already had a nice knife. I was more than a little bit hopeful that he would give it to me. He did not.

That evening, when I was bemoaning my bad luck (and Billy's good luck!), Mom tried to cheer me up, saying, "Well, Kenny, maybe it's just as well. You might cut yourself with it." Needless to say, that didn't help at all. I still wished I could have been the lucky guy who found the knife.

One morning, about a month or so later, when I arrived at school, friend Billy came up to me with his hands behind his back. I listened with eager anticipation as he delivered his brief speech: "Kenny, I already have a knife, so I've decided to give you the one I found." With that he brought his hands around and handed me his belated gift. I would not have recognized it as the same knife. The sheath was shrunken, cracked, and warped from obviously having been left out in the rain or snow. The point was broken off of the now pitted, rusty blade. Moreover, it had several deep nicks in it. One side of the handle grip was gone, leaving only a couple bent rivets.

I did my best to show appreciation. I tried to tell myself that a crummy, beat-up knife was better than no knife at all. But I could never fully convince myself of that. Thinking back on it now, I cannot for the life of me remember whatever became of that belated gift. I could never feel really attached to it because it always seemed to be moaning: *If only, if only, if only*—

I'm glad we learn from the Holy Scriptures that the Lord Jesus Christ is pleased when people—young or old, even all bent and broken—come to Him. I do not know if *He* ever thinks, *If only, if only, if only*, but I do know that He said, "Suffer little children, and forbid them not to come unto me, for of such is the kingdom of heaven" (Matt. 19:14). I know also that, in *His* eyes, we are all, in one sense or another, "children." Thus, it can never be too late to give Him our finest gift—the gift of our love and devotion—yes, even if it is belated.

On a few occasions, down through the years, I have felt impressed to tell this story—usually in talks to young people. As of last September, I can now add a rather touching, heartwarming "P. S."

I was once again privileged (and challenged!) to serve as pastor-chaplain at an "Outdoor School" with 100 or so primarily fifth- and sixth-grade children in attendance. At one of the evening chapel devotionals, I told this belated gift knife story. After the service, as we were somewhat crowded together moving back down the path in the semi-darkness toward our cabins, a little fellow pushed his way to my side and shoved a small hard object into my hand. If he said anything, I didn't hear it. He then hurried off to join his buddies on down the trail. When I came under a light, I saw that the small object he gave me was a cute little pocket knife.

Since kids were frequently losing things that were later found, then announced and held up at various meetings and later reclaimed by their owners, I assumed that he probably had found the knife and expected me to locate its rightful owner. I quickened my pace, and when I caught up with him, I asked, "Son, did you find this knife and want me to announce it at the morning meeting?" He seemed surprised and perhaps a bit timid as he softly replied, "Oh, no, Pastor Campbell—I gave it to you."

Many years ago, I was a very small, very poor lad. I vividly remember how precious a pocket knife can be to a small lad. I do not know if the little fellow who gave me his knife feels the same way, but this I know for certain: I now own many knives, including a hunting knife an uncle gave me about sixty years ago when I was a teenager and another knife my long-time buddy, Jim Homburg, gave me only a few months ago. Monetarily speaking, most of these knives are worth much more than the one that sympathetic, tender-hearted little guy gave me last September.

But … Chandler, I will always treasure your kind, thoughtful, extremely timely gift.

4.
Snow Potpourri

The first few years of my life were spent in a sunny area of California. Consequently, I never saw snow until I was seven years old. It has been a cause of intrigue, delight, and, at times, disgust ever since.

We moved from California during the winter of 1938. I don't remember the exact month, but engraved into my memory bank is a vivid picture of huge mounds of snow in towns we went through. I remember trees that had limbs that hung low from the weight of the snow they carried.

Once, an oncoming car went into a spin on the icy highway. It switched ends, lanes, and directions several times then concluded the grand performance by skidding into our lane. No harm was done, however, since it then sped along in front of us, now traveling in the same direction we were taking. Thinking back on it now, I imagine Dad was shaking with fright because of a near accident, but I was naive and delighted. I kept hoping another car would put on another splendid show for me!

I had never seen tall rubber overshoes (galoshes) with metal buckles. Many of the men we saw—and most of the boys my size—didn't bother to fasten the buckles. As they sauntered along, the metal buckles slapped each other making a tinkling clicking sound. I longed for the day when I too could march proudly along with my own personal noise makers. (Sad to say, I later learned this was not as glamorous as I thought. They can trip you and cause injury and—even worse—embarrassment when you fall on your face in front of others—especially the girls you are trying to impress with your manliness.)

When we, at last, arrived at our destination—North Pine Creek and Lemanasky Lake in the high country, about twenty miles west of Tonasket, Washington—the natives all agreed that it was the worst winter they had experienced in many years. Indeed, the last few miles were on a large bobsled pulled by a team of horses struggling along through snow so deep that it covered most of the fence posts. I thought it was glorious fun at the time, but I learned later that it is not fun when the wind is blowing and the thermometer reads below zero!

I was captivated and astounded by my older country cousins, the Hall kids. They took long boards, laboriously planed them smooth, then boiled one end of them for many hours in a big laundry wash tub on their mom's wood burning cook stove. Next, they put them in a simple but effective homemade press of sorts. This eventually bent the boiled ends up—a little. Finally, they nailed sturdy leather straps onto them, straps which—more or less (often less)—held them onto their feet. Lastly, much to my amazement and delight, they attempted to stand on them while coasting speedily down steep hills! Sometimes they actually succeeded, but mostly they fell over backwards and plowed deep holes or furrows in the snow with their fannies. Sometimes they fell forwards and came up looking like snowmen, except that they were spitting out snow and trying to brush it out of their eyes and nose with their bulky, clumsy mittens. I liked that part a lot, but Cousin Dick did even better.

Becoming bored with merely coasting down hills with boards strapped to their feet the cousins decided to add to the challenge. They took scoop shovels and piled up a high mound of snow about halfway down the hill. Yep—a ski jump! We all, with eager anticipation, watched as Cousin Dick sped full throttle down the hill. He hit the jump dead center and sailed gracefully into the sky—only to dive back down head-first into the deep, soft snow. All we could see of him were his legs waving frantically in the breeze. Ah! It was hilarious (for the spectators)!

> *All we could see of him were his legs waving frantically in the breeze.*

Sledding was lots of fun, although, generally speaking, we first had to tromp the deep, soft snow down, otherwise our sleds just sunk down into the snow and refused to budge. Occasionally the weather would get warm enough for the snow to begin to melt, then it would suddenly turn really cold again. This froze the top layer of snow, making it hard and slick as ice. We could walk on this crust, and our sleds went delightfully fast. This was great sport, *but*—all too often when you were going about fifty miles per hour (or so it seemed)—your sled runners would break through the crust. This caused a very abrupt halt. You suddenly found yourself off your sled skidding speedily along on your belly and face! Rub a piece of coarse sandpaper up and down your face with emphasis on your nose if you'd like to get a good idea of what I'm attempting to describe.

One time, a neighbor gave us a sickly little "bummer" lamb. The lamb's mommy had refused to accept him, so we "adopted" him. We fed him with a bottle, and nursed him 'til he was healthy and strong. He grew to be mischievous, boisterous, and lovable—kind of like Li'l Abner of comic strip fame, so we named him "Abner."

We kids got down on all fours and taught him the gentle game of head butting. Much to our delight, he proved to be a fast learner. He took the game quite seriously. In fact, as he grew into a big, burly fellow, his love for the game of head butting became a trifle too serious.

Like "Mary's Little Lamb," Abner followed us to school whenever he got the chance. And so it came to pass that, one fine sunny winter day, when the snow was deep and soft and wet and muddy, our dear gentle friend, Mrs. Bigelow, walked with her children to school. As she was leaving the school yard, she noticed that one of her galoshes was unfastened. She bent over to fasten it, and the next thing she felt was a tremendous battering thrust to her behind! When she, at last, struggled to get her disgruntled and soggy self up out of a large snow bank, there stood Abner with what she insisted was "a grin on his face." She further reported that he seemed not in the least bit ashamed or "sheepish" for having committed such a dastardly deed, in fact, his neck was stiffly arched and cocked ready for a second round at his favorite game. Kindly, Mrs. Bigelow confessed that it took many loud, shrill screams spiced up with some words she taught her children never to use to convince Abner that she did not wish to play with him anymore.

Abner was too much a part of our family for even tough ol' Dad to butcher. When spring came, he took him to the livestock auction in Tonasket. We presume that Abner became a bigamist and sired many little Abners and Abneretts, and is now in sheep heaven—at least we can hope that's where he went.

This year I am, once again, writing from my little hideaway, high in the mountains of Pine Creek where all of this took place. It is mid-November. I had heard the snow had come early here this year, but I never realized how much. It took me about three and a half hours to drive from home at Deer Park to North Pine Creek, a distance of about 165 miles. It then took about two and a half hours to battle my way about a half mile through snow two to three feet deep from the "main" road, which is quite primitive, on into my rustic abode!

Some people accuse me of being crazy (especially at my "advanced" age!) to put myself and my 4x4 Ford Explorer through such stress and hard work and misery for the sake of just being here, but they do not understand.

Last night I hiked—no, wallowed—through the snow up a mountain to find a spot where my cellphone would work. (I wanted to assure my wife, Eleanor, that the cougars had not eaten me—yet.) It was an awesomely lovely evening. Bright moon-beams were dancing across the sparkling snow. The magic of my beloved mountains still works. Once again, at least in my mind, I was young—sledding, and skiing, and ice skating with much-loved friends and family. These hills still echo with the sound of our laughter and our shouts of pure, innocent joy. It's so good to be home again.

Or am I?

Are we ever *truly home* when we are "home"?

How well I remember that exciting, miserable ordeal of going to and from town in the dead of winter when we lived here at Lemanasky Lake year-round. It was long before plowed roads and four-wheel drive vehicles. Even when chained up, weighted-down pickups could no longer navigate the steep, snow-clogged, narrow roads. They had to be left far down at the bottom of the treacherous, dangerous Wingo Hill. Or in the other direction, at the Beeman School. We and the other North Pine Creekers had to travel to our vehicles by means of teams and sleds.

Dad built a small version of a horse drawn bobsled by using only the front "bob" with tongue attached. He built a large wooden box on it to haul passengers, groceries, and "whatever." It pulled easier than a complete four-runner bobsled, but it still was an awful load for the horses as they struggled to pull it up the horrendous, often snow-drifted Wingo Hill. The poor critters had to stop every few yards to catch their breath with sides heaving and hearts pounding.

While the horses sweated, with steam actually rising from them because of their exertion, we froze. I mean that almost literally. Often we fellows would get off and wallow up to the crotch through snow for a while to lighten the load, but tough and hardy, as we may have been, we couldn't go far before we were totally exhausted.

Little Sis Sherry was only four or five years old, and much too small and fragile to be expected to get out and walk. One particular ordeal of a trip up the hill stands out in our memory. It was bitterly cold, dark, and miserable. Little Sis was huddled down in the dirty, scratchy hay with an old blanket over her. But she was still so cold that her teeth chattered and her small body shivered uncontrollably. Her weak voice quavered so badly she could scarcely speak. After a while, however, she softly announced, "I'm feelin' better now, Dad—I'm getting warm."

Dad immediately stopped the team, and in a voice which sounded both stern and alarmed commanded Sis to get out and walk. She whimpered and fussed and pleaded and cried, but it only made Dad more insistent and urgent. Sis got out and walked as best she could. Brother Garry and I thought Dad was awful mean, but, as he explained later, this very well may have saved her life. She had shown all the signs of hypothermia and of being frozen to death.

Little Sis was huddled down in the dirty, scratchy hay with an old blanket over her. But she was still so cold that her teeth chattered and her small body shivered uncontrollably.

Family and friends, hear me well now: We are not truly home yet. If we are getting too warm, too comfortable in this tired, dangerous old world, it may be because we are in danger of spiritual hypothermia and death. Let us be certain that we are walking with the Lord Jesus Christ—now and always.

5.
The Lesson

I am aware that there is considerable discussion as to the ideal age at which a child should begin his or her formal education. My parents felt that I should take in a bit of kindergarten at age six, and then, providing I didn't flunk clay class, I could begin first grade at age seven. I disagreed. Big Brother Stan was already in the second grade, and I didn't like being left behind. I decided that I should just skip kindergarten and first grade and join Stan in second grade on the sly. (At that time we were living in Sunnyvale, California.)

I watched for my chance, and it wasn't long in coming. One fine morning when mom was busy in another room and Stan headed out for his walk to school, I sneaked out the door and followed him. I stayed back a ways and availed myself of trees and hedges so he would not realize he was being followed. With my five-year-old brain, I "reasoned" that, when I arrived at school, the teacher would be pleased to see me. She would promptly enroll me in second grade. Stan, Mom, and Dad would all be proud of me, and all would be well.

Stan's route took us by the train depot and across several railroad tracks. I had been by there before but usually just hurrying along in the car and always with Mom or Dad. This was different and exciting, and I got "side-tracked" and forgot all about my desire for higher education.

I began to do what most kids like to do, I tried walking on the rails, and I attempted to jump from one railroad tie to the next. The strange aroma of the creosote, the pleasant sunny day, and the scary but captivating thrill of being "on my own" were hypnotic.

After a while, I was intrigued by something I hadn't notice at first. The iron rails seemed to be vibrating and making my feet feel tingly. I was fascinated and puzzled by the mysterious sensation. I didn't have long to ponder that matter. A frightening monster suddenly came thundering around a curve from behind the depot building. It was shrieking, and smoke was belching out of it's top. Huge clouds of steam hissed loudly out each side. My feet no longer merely tingled, they shook!

No doubt you've heard the term, "paralyzed with fear." It's real! I think what happens is that our mind goes into "overload" and becomes incapable of sending signals to our hands and feet. It was not so much that I couldn't move, it was more that I couldn't even *think* to move.

> *No doubt you've heard the term, "paralyzed with fear."*

Suddenly I was snatched off the track, and the next thing I became aware of was a large black lady vigorously slapping my fanny with the palm of her hand! I speedily "awoke" from my hypnotic like state and began to squall and bawl. Moments later Mom dashed up with her panting and crying and laughing all mixed up together.

And what do you suppose was the first thing I said to her? Pointing an angry, accusing finger at my savior I blubbered, *"She spanked me!"* And what did Mom do? She hugged the black lady (angels are not always white you know) and thanked her, then she sternly pointed me toward home. It was a speedy trip. With Mom whacking my bottom about every other step, I set a lively pace indeed!

I didn't make it to school on that long ago day, but I learned some valuable lessons, nonetheless.

How close was the train? I do not remember. Would I have come to my senses before it could hit me? I don't know. Was the black lady a "flesh and blood" human "angel," or was she actually a genuine heavenly angel? I don't know. *But*——it is sadly humorous that my primary five-year-old reaction that day was, *"She spanked me!"* Never mind that she very well may have saved my life. *"She spanked me!"* That's all that registered.

Add a big seventy to the five and you will be close to guessing my age at this writing. I suspect that most of you who are reading or hearing this are also more than five years old. I wonder how many times our Savior will have to "spank us" and snatch us off the devil's track in His loving desire to save our lives, not merely for the "here and now" but, much more importantly, for eternity as well.

Now no chastening for the present seemeth to be joyous, but grievous: nevertheless afterward it yieldeth the peaceable fruit of righteousness unto them which are exercised thereby. Wherefore lift up the hands which hang down, and the feeble knees; and make straight paths for your feet, lest that which is lame be turned out of the way; but let it rather be healed. Follow peace with all men, and holiness, without which no man shall see the Lord. (Heb. 12:11–14)

6.

The Basement

Picture, if you will, a snug, cozy little cottage nestled in a lush green meadow at the edge of a small peaceful lake. The tranquil scene is enhanced by the forested mountains that stand at attention all around it. It is evening, and the yellow glow of a kerosene lamp softly beckons from the glistening windows of the charming abode. *There!* Now that I have indulged my feeble attempt at waxing "romantic and eloquent," I shall proceed to tell it as it actually was (or, at least, as I remember it after sixty-eight years or so).

As a small child I certainly did not think of our little house at Lemanasky Lake as being a shack. Granted, if it still existed and if I could see it again now, I might appraise it much more critically. Another thing—the soft mellow glow of a kerosene lamp may set a "romantical mood," but expect to do some serious squinting when you attempt to read or write by it!

(I was reminded of this when the R.V. battery I use for lights and other things here in my Pine Creek hideout "mansion"—ha!—died last night, and I had to dig out my "for emergency use only" kerosene lamp.)

Dim kerosene lamps were, however, the least of our worries those many years ago. The real problem was the lake. It insisted upon flooding the meadow and surrounding the house. In fact, when the snow melted in the springtime, and the beavers dammed up the Pine Creek overflow, the lake threatened to move right on into the house. Having a house *at* the lake may be pleasant, but having a lake *in* the house is not!

When the snow melted in the springtime, and the beavers dammed up the Pine Creek overflow, the lake threatened to move right on into the house.

One day when I came home from school I was intrigued and puzzled by what Dad was doing. He had the team hitched to a big scoop shovel looking affair with two sturdy handles. (He called it a "Fresno.") He had gouged a large hole in a knoll several yards from the house. As I watched, Dad and the team continued to make the hole ever larger.

When he, at last, yelled, "Whoa," and stopped the horses—and himself—for a "breather," I excitedly and hopefully asked, "Are ya diggin' a mine, Dad?"

"Nope, I'm diggin' a basement," he answered.

I knew only a little more than nothing about building, but I did know that a basement ought to have a house over it, so my next question was a natural.

"Wow! Dad. Are ya gonna build us a new house?"

"No, Kenny. We're going to put our old house on top of it."

I was quite certain Dad was kidding me. In my mind that would be impossible, but to go along with his gag I asked, "How're ya gonna do that?"

Dad's answer was short and mystifying, "You'll see, Son, you'll see." And, with that, he started the team with a quick shake of the lines and went back to his digging.

The long days became weeks, and the busy weeks became months. Beside the usual hard work of ranching Dad slaved away on the basement project, working early and late. We were excited to learn that ours was not to be a mere dark, low ceiling basement. No, indeed. Dad enthusiastically declared that it was to be a daylight basement with windows and a door. Big Brother Stan and I would have our very own room with a stove, and we could move out of the attic.

Mom would have her longed-for fruit room with shelves, and there would even be another small area where she could do the washing. Since the washing machine had a gasoline engine, Dad promised to make a special hole through an outside wall and route the exhaust pipe through it. Mom would then no longer have to push and pull the clumsy washing machine outside to use it. She'd be able to wash clothes just downstairs in the comfort of our new daylight basement.

Mind you, we had no electricity. Dad had no timesaving, labor-saving power tools. Many yards of concrete had to be mixed by hand in a mortar box. All the sawing of boards had to be done with a hand saw.

I wasn't the only one who wondered how Dad could move the house many yards across a spongy meadow, up a steep rise, and then lift it up to, at last, place it squarely over the daylight basement. We later learned that the project was the skeptical talk of our small neighborhood.

I truly wish I could remember exactly how Dad performed the miracle of engineering. All I recall is that it involved a team of horses, the faithful little 1936 Chevy pickup, one medium-size screw jack, chains and a lot of cable, many large pulleys attached to trees, and "scads" of timbers and rollers cut from trees.

I also remember that Dad used more than his usual amount of "snoose" (a nickname for Copenhagen chewing tobacco), and also threw in more than a few "spicy words" during the process. For her part, Mom did a lot of crying, a little screaming, and, knowing her, she almost certainly speeded many silent prayers up to heaven.

Stan and I did the scary part. When team driving, Dad shouted the dreaded command, we hunched down under the tilted house and placed wooden wedges behind the rollers to prevent the house from rolling backward. Dad could then unhook the team and rig up for another pull.

I well remember what a happy day it was when, at long last, the house sat proudly upon its new daylight basement. It was finally out of the cruel grasp of Lemanasky's wet fingers. Late autumn had now arrived, but the most difficult and important part was over. During the long winter months, Dad dreamed and happily sketched plans for the finish work he intended to do "come spring," as he put it.

Spring came, as it always does. Old Lemanasky overflowed its banks, as it usually does, but it couldn't reach our snug home perched high and dry on its brand-new daylight basement. But— brace yourself—now comes the sad, all-too-true end to this story.

Water began to seep through the cement walls and ooze up through the still dirt floor of the "daylight basement." There was no stopping it. It seems that Dad had dug nearly into an underground spring. The small drips and tiny trickles soon joined together to become a fair-sized creek.

As the creek flowed steadily out of our eagerly anticipated daylight basement it washed our fond dreams away with it.

Dad wryly observed that, "A well with a pump in the basement would be nice to have but an actual free-flowing creek down there is quite another matter." It was not long before he declared the house unsafe to live in with its crumbled basement foundation. Later we tore it down and used the lumber and other materials to build a shop at another place we bought farther down the mountain.

Macho Dad was not a crying man, but thinking about it just now I can't remember him talking much, if at all, about the basement fiasco. Perhaps his disappointment and sense of loss was so great that he couldn't bear to talk about it. Some things and some people are like that you know.

Just now I am thinking of another Father who has been and *is* now involved in a "project" of infinitely greater importance than any daylight basement.

> For God so loved the world that He gave His only begotten Son, that whosoever believeth in Him should not perish, but have everlasting life. For God sent not His Son into the world to condemn the world; but that the world, through Him might be saved. (John 3:16–17)

Sadly, the Bible informs us that multitudes will not allow God the Father to save them through His divine Son, Jesus Christ. The Bible, likewise, tells us of a time in the not-so-distant future when

God will "wipe away all tears" from the eyes of His beloved people (Rev. 21:4). He has, in effect, given His all to save not just "the world" but individuals. Will He not then suffer immeasurable disappointment and grief over those who choose to be forever lost? And, pray tell, who will wipe away the tears of God, the tears He will shed over those who shun His invitation to live eternally with Him? And it won't be in a mere daylight basement. No, indeed. It will be a "city which hath foundations, whose builder and maker is God" Himself (Heb. 11:10)!

Let *us* not disappoint God.

7.

When I Wore Armor

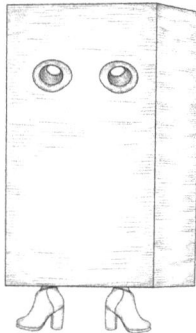

The fact that I vividly remember the big cardboard box but can't recall what came in it attests to my attachment to it. My frugal Dad usually found some practical use for 'most anything and everything, so the fact that he allowed me to "adopt" it for my very own was, of itself, rather unusual. Perhaps he got a kick from watching some of my adventuring with it and just didn't have the heart to put it to some mundane use.

The box was long and narrow, and, when I dropped it down over me, it came down to my ankles. I considered it to be a perfect fit. After I walked around blindly bumping into things for a while, good ol' Dad measured me up and cut eye-holes in the box.

Evidently it was a magic box because, when I strutted around the yard in it, I suddenly became invincible—or so I thought. I was intrigued by pictures of knights in armor in one of my school books, so it was easy to imagine that, when I was in the box, I had my armor on and was protected from nearly any danger.

Evidently it was a magic box because, when I strutted around the yard in it, I suddenly became invincible—or so I thought.

We had a big old red rooster who pretty much had me "buffaloed," as the old saying goes. I dreaded gathering the eggs because the chore often involved getting my hind end pecked or my legs flogged by Big Red. It was most embarrassing since I tried to be macho like Dad.

I was delighted to discover that, when I had my armor on, Big Red was just another big chicken—read that as just a big sissy. Squawking like an old hen, he ran for the bushes at full speed with wings flapping. It was most satisfying—for me. *Ah! The joy of wearing armor!*

Since Big Red and his harem were so excited by my armor, I decided to show it to the milk cows. They were in the corral just loafing around eating hay and chewing their cuds. When they saw me coming, they all bunched up in the far corner and watched with bulging eyes. Then they tried to back over each other in efforts to get away from the mysterious walking, talking, monster box. I was so pleased by their rapt attention that I forgot all about our young bull over in another corner behind me. He was busily serving an apprenticeship with the goal of soon becoming a bigamist and making love to a bunch of heifers.

Suddenly I heard Dad yell, "Kenny, get the *BLANK* out of there with that *BLANKITY* box!" Whenever Dad yelled, I made haste to obey. This time it was not easy in view of the short choppy steps I had to take with the box down around my ankles. Also, at a faster speed, it bounced up and down, making the eyeholes line up with my eyes for only a second or two every now and then.

When I was safely out of the corral Dad told me that the little bull had been pawing the ground with his head down and was just about to charge me. Granted, I was foolish and naïve, but not enough to cause me to believe that my cardboard "armor" could protect me from the thrust of an angry, charging 600-pound young bull.

I do not remember Dad's exact words, but he firmly suggested that the chickens and the cows might not see the humor in my armor act and might retaliate by cutting way back on their production of eggs and milk. He further advised that, from henceforth, I should confine my entertaining armor act to Tippy the family dog, to the cats, and maybe to certain people. Since, he even raised the possibility—and not so tactfully—of repossessing my armor, I knew that, as usual, Dad was quite serious.

It was a lot of fun being in the box while other kids—preferably small ones—whacked it with sticks and threw rocks at me. On rare occasions, I succumbed to bribery or begging and generously allowed some school chum to don my armor. I kind of enjoyed being a "hitter" rather than the "hittee" for a change.

But, alas, such harsh treatment, along with rain and later some snowballs, eventually took their toll. I, at last, had to admit that my "armor" wasn't merely tarnished—it was tattered and torn and done for. This was twice sad because I had not yet lived long enough to have outgrown its pretended magic. The final contribution to the Campbell family, by my precious "armor," was the heat it produced upon the occasion of its cremation service in the living room stove. It was, indeed, a sad parting, and I missed it greatly—for a few days.

I was by no means the only kid who ever had fun with a large cardboard box. I have observed that this seems to be a natural instinct for children and for kittens. Could it be that God made us this way? Do we all crave protection such as that provided by some sort of physical or mental armor? I think so.

Listen now to some things God has to say about armor, as recorded in the New Testament book of Ephesians, in the Holy

Bible: "Put on the whole armour of God, that ye may be able to stand against the wiles of the devil" (Eph. 6:11). "Wherefore take unto you the whole armour of God, that ye may be able to withstand in the evil day, and having done all, to stand. Stand, therefore having your loins girt about with truth, and having on the breastplate of righteousness: and your feet shod with the preparation of the gospel of peace; above all, taking the shield of faith, wherewith ye shall be able to quench all the fiery darts of the wicked. And take the helmet of salvation, and the sword of the Spirit, which is the word of God" (Eph. 6:13–17).

Whenever I read and contemplate these blessed words of Scripture, I remember my flimsy cardboard "armor." By contrast, GOD'S armor will never wear out. It is good for eternity!

Ah! The joy of wearing armor!

8.

The Bronc Buster

It all took place well over seventy-five years ago, so I suppose it's little wonder that I've forgotten exactly where I got the idea, much less the mental picture I came up with at that time. In any event, it set me up for a surprise—a surprise that, at first, was disappointing but that, in the end, turned out just fine.

It seemed to me that Dad could do almost anything that needed doing around the ranch, thus my first surprise came when he announced that he was going to hire a horse breaker to, at least, "green break" three-year-old, skittish, Roman-nosed Franky. Dad said he had too much to do besides spending precious time messing with a semi-wild cayuse. Besides that, he couldn't risk getting banged up and being unable to do more important work.

Our eagerly looked forward to attendance at local rodeos once or twice a year was about the only activity that we enjoyed off the ranch—that and fishing. But fishing hardly counted since we lived nearly on the banks of Lemanasky Lake. Moreover, fish were, more or less, part of our usual diet. Thus, at times, it seemed difficult to decide whether fishing was for fun or simply yet another chore which had to be taken care of.

But ... a bronc buster coming to our ranch? That, for certain, was exciting news! Not only did I think I knew what he would look like, I also was fairly sure I knew what he would do, and what would happen. No actual surprise there, or so I thought.

The bronc buster couldn't tell Dad even the exact day he could come, so, whenever I could, I looked down the road or just stood quietly and listened for the sound of a fast-galloping horse. The big black stallion would come charging around the corner in a cloud of dust. I'd just stand my ground to show I was no greenhorn easily scared. The bronc buster would smoothly dismount like a skilled rodeo calf roper even before his showy mount skidded to a stop.

The handsome rider would tip his perfectly blocked Stetson to me just like I was a grown man worthy of such cowboy courtesy. Then he'd ask, "Is this the Campbell ranch?" His expensive chaps would, of course, sport the brand of the outfit he mostly rode for. He'd be wearing—in low, quick-draw fashion—two long barrel six guns with pearly white butts. His silver buckled cartridge belt would be fully stocked with no nonsense .45 caliber bullets.

I would judge him to be about twenty-five years old. Dad and Mom were about thirty at that time, and they were real old! (*Boy*— was I ever in for the surprises that would come later!)

The young bronc buster I imagined coming would make quick, short work with wild, spooky, cantankerous Franky. He would snug him up tight and close to a good solid corral post and then saddle him up using a special saddle with bucking rolls. He would climb aboard taking a few moments to scrunch himself tight in the saddle and mentally steel himself for the jarring he expected. After all, he was a professional rider, a bronc buster.

He would signal for Dad—or hopefully me—to turn Franky loose, and then Franky would buck and whirl, rear and fish tail, dip low, and then circle the corral, all the while grunting and making crude, naughty, snorting noises. But the bronc buster would just sit tight in the saddle without even losing his hat, much less grabbing the horn or pullin' leather. After a few minutes of such strenuous activity, Franky would be slowing down, breathing hard, and doing more running than bucking, at which point the modestly cocky, victorious bronc buster would yell, "Open the gate!" Still wearing only the halter, Franky and rider would lunge out of the corral to speedily disappear in a cloud of dust around the first curve of the country road.

About thirty minutes or so later (in my daydreams!), Franky would come leisurely trotting back—like a good ol' cow horse should. Just as though he had been "born again." The bronc buster would hand Dad the lead rope and say, "There you go, Clarence. He's green broke now. You can take it from here. He's a good horse with a smooth, easy gait. That'll be twenty bucks."

Yeah—all this in my nine- or ten-year-old dreams and imagination. Was I ever in for a surprise!

One day an old guy came moseying down our road on an ancient appearing nag.

One day an old guy came moseying down our road on an ancient appearing nag. Much to my surprise and disappointment, *he* was the bronc buster! His hat—if you could call it that—might have been a cowboy hat sometime in the distant past, but it was so beat up and misshapen it would have been a wild guess as to what it had been to start. He wore no chaps, and his faded pants were baggy and loose fitting. Still worse, they hung rather low beneath a bulging belly, anchored in place rather precariously by a strand of binder twine.

He sported no sidearm, but I gave him a mite of respect on account of a wrinkled and warped leather scabbard tied to his weather-beaten old saddle. From it protruded the faded, scratched, gouged up stock of some kind of rifle.

His boots—with no spurs—may have been my greatest cause for disappointment and alarm. They looked to be some kind of collusion (or collision!) between the shoes of a logger, a trapper, and a hiker. They even had leather laces. To their credit, they, at least, had high heels.

After the usual expected polite protocol, which involved considerable tobacco smoking, chewing, and spitting, Dad and Bill at long last trudged out to the corral. I, of course tagged along behind, as did little brother Garry who was just a toddler.

A little side path here: Not long before this, Mom, being busy one day, suddenly discovered—with much alarm—that Garry was missing. After a few minutes of frantic searching, she ran to the corral. There she found him, sitting right at the hind hooves of a rather easily spooked horse. Garry was calmly sitting there, playing in the dirt and humming to himself! Mom very softly convinced him to come over to her. She later said that, evidently, Garry had a guarding angel who had a way with horses.

Dad and ol' Bill just stood leaning on the top corral rail gabbing and gazing thoughtfully at Franky, the "guest of honor." Finally, Bill the bronc buster went to his horse and got his lariat. I thought, *Good! At last we'll see some action!* But mostly it was yet another disappointing surprise for me—at least, at first. Bill climbed over the top rail and just stood still there in the middle of the corral for what seemed to me about half of eternity. Franky, with wild eyes, galloped around and around and back and forth snorting and trying to keep an eye on Bill. He, at last, stopped for a breather as instinct forced him to show curiosity about that strange guy who just stood there watching him. Then Bill began to twirl the loop of his lariat, and Franky proceeded with his merry-go-round business.

Then, so fast I couldn't see what happened, the bronc buster's loop shot out and Franky was on the ground trying to get up. But it was all to no avail. Old Bill's deftness, skill, and speed were akin to that of a top calf roper at a rodeo. He had tied Franky in a way that caused him to fall back down every time he tried to get back up on his feet. There was no cussing, no loud yelling, and Franky wasn't hurt. Bill spent a lot of time down on his knees talking softly to Franky and gently petting and patting him. I was surprised and pleased.

Most of you who read or hear this true story are not so naïve as to believe that this one "treatment" was all it took to "break" Franky. Rather, it took several such "treatments" over several days. I and even little brother Garry were honored by ol' Bill to be his little helper "bronc busters." After a couple days and a few more "treatments," we could crawl all over Franky, and he wouldn't tremble or shake or even try to get up. We even tapped him lightly here and there with rolled up newspaper, and he showed no fear. Bill had us drag a saddle blanket back and forth over him, even over his head until he didn't even flinch.

To be sure, when Bill at last put the pad on Franky and a little later added the saddle for the first time, Franky did a little dancing and prancing around. There was, however, no "rodeo" like I had expected (and quite honestly, at first had secretly hoped for!). In just a few days, ol' Bill was leading Franky around with me sitting proudly in the saddle.

After the few days he spent with us, the bronc buster had to leave. I hated to see him go. I no longer cared that he didn't wear chaps or a well-shaped cowboy hat, or six guns, or even real cowboy boots with flashy silver spurs. I didn't care that his mount was a rather mundane ancient nag and not a big, black spirited stallion.

So when he shook hands with Dad and then stooped down and shook my hand and patted me on the shoulder, thanking me for helping him in breaking Franky, I fought back tears—just like the little kid that I actually was.

I watched as my friend the bronc buster and his old nag disappeared around the corner. Yes, I hated to see him go, and, to my knowledge and memory, I never saw him again. I wonder—would he be surprised and pleased by the pleasant memories he left with me?

Now, without sounding too "preachy," it seems to me that these two somewhat differing methods of horse "breaking" to some small degree may be used to illustrate how God deals with us—at least the way in which we as individuals perceive Him doing.

There are those who think of God being forceful and dictatorial. According to their thinking, He breaks us down until we rather grudgingly "comply," primarily out of fear to do otherwise. Granted, my putting it as I have may be a bit exaggerated, but I have encountered people in conversation who revealed such a concept of God and His methods.

Yes, I admit that, by picking and choosing and ignoring context, one can come up with such a distorted, mistaken idea of God. But how reliable and trustworthy do you suppose Franky would have been if he had been "green broke" by my first imagined bronc buster in this story?

It is also true that in this story, as it actually transpired, ol' Bill had to put Franky down on the ground several times. But he did this so that he could comfort and pet and gentle him down. *The wild horse had to learn to trust us before we could feel confident in trusting him.*

In my humble opinion and experience, I am convinced that this method of training more accurately portrays God's dealing with us than does the "bronc buster" approach. (When it comes to what you do with your horse, I must leave it up to your wise, God-led discretion.)

Jesus says, "Take my yoke [or maybe my saddle] upon you, and learn of me; for I am meek and lowly in heart: and ye shall find rest unto your souls. For my yoke is easy, and my burden is light" (Matt. 11:29–30).

"Close the Gate!"

I don't remember exactly how they made their escape, and it's not important anyway, but two of our horses were missing. We searched high and low for them on our home ranch, but to no avail. Then, one day, a neighbor told us that there was a herd of semi-wild horses running free down in the Horse Spring Coulee country eight or ten miles from our home ranch. When we described our horses he said he couldn't be certain, but there were a couple down there that might be ours.

A little scouting expedition with the old pickup truck confirmed that our horses were there. It also confirmed what we feared. Since the rascals were never easy to catch even when by themselves in their "home turf," there was no way we'd ever lay hands on them now that they were galloping around over thousands of acres of rangeland with a band of undomesticated mavericks. We realized that it would be a difficult task for just Dad and I astride speedy saddle horses.

A few days later, Dad and I saddled up very early in the morning and headed down to Horse Spring Coulee. By the time we reached the area and located the horses, our poor mounts had already covered a lot of miles. Moreover, it was a miserably hot day besides.

We all too well knew the challenge facing us, but one thing was in our favor. Located in the vast open range was a large corral with a heavy, sturdy board gate. It was a big "if," but *if* we could drive the wise, spooky horses into the corral and get the gate shut, we would have it made.

It wasn't long before we discovered that some of the wild horses were faster than our saddle horses and practically tireless. We raced up and down, back and forth, and around and around the huge level range. The wild rascals acted like they were truly enjoying being chased! Every now and then, we'd get our hopes up as some of the lead horses seemed to be heading for the opening into the corral. Then, at the last moment, they would veer out around it. It was so disappointing and aggravating! Dad had yelled, "Since you're younger and your horse is faster, if they ever run into the corral, you jump off and get the gate shut before they realize they're trapped!"

And so it went for what seemed like—and probably was— *hours!* Then, at long last, just when we were beginning to fear it would never happen, several of the horses along with ours galloped into the corral. I was about fifty feet behind and skidded Raven to somewhat of a stop before I hit the ground running full throttle. In a second or three, I reached the gate. The adrenalin was flowing, and I never even noticed the weight of the massive gate *until* … and the rest is a daze!

The gate was mere inches from where it would have locked into its sturdy, iron latch. Suddenly, I felt a crashing, crushing blow that I cannot adequately describe. Then I saw a lot of stars and colors, and then darkness. The next thing I was aware of was that I was several feet from the gate and flat on my back. My entire face and nose felt numb. When I reached up to feel my face, the sensation was as though a dentist had given it about a dozen hefty shots of extra powerful Novocain, and blood was flowing freely.

You've guessed what happened, haven't you? My puny weight against the gate was no match for the several thousand pounds force of the horses as they charged full speed into the gate from the other side!

It sounds funny now, some sixty plus years later, but I actually believed my entire face was gone! Macho Dad sympathetically assured me that, as best he could tell through all the blood, my face was still there. As I recall, it was several days before my face "thawed out" and felt semi-normal again.

(I presume the painful incident never did any permanent damage to my face. At least that's my firm opinion, despite what some of you wisecrackers would have us believe! *Ha!*)

"What of your escaped horses?" you ask. Real cowboys seldom give up. After a few minutes, I and my numb face and aching body remounted, and, before that long day was quite over, in fact, at dusk we finally ran the horses into the corral again. It was even more difficult and time consuming the second time, but, this time, *we* got the gate shut. All during that long, exasperating ordeal, I kept thinking how much trouble, frustration, and *pain* would have been avoided if only I had succeeded in closing the gate on those wild beasts at the outset.

Surely there is a solid lesson there for *many* aspects of life, wouldn't you agree?

10.
The Hat

I thought I had myself sufficiently steeled to carry through with the dreaded task, but when I raised the lid of the trash can, I just couldn't do it. How could I relegate to a dark, stinking trash can an old friend that had served me so faithfully for so many years?! Oh, to be sure, it was bruised and battered and literally falling apart, but, even so, it was chock-full of memories—good and bad—of the many years we have spent together.

It was never designed to serve as a helmet, but, nonetheless, it valiantly took most of the blow for my noggin those too frequent times when I stupidly and hastily reared up under some immovable object which was too low for my head. This largely accounts for the ripped, broken, dented, and torn loose crown of my cherished old hat. I was always saddened by such injuries to my previously flawless straw hat, but, as a genuine Durango cowboy model, perhaps it expected some rough rides. Better it than my head! All of which reminds me—

Several friends and I were doing a little "bush-whacking," taking a supposed short-cut to a trail shown on our map. The terrain was steep and precipitous with many low hanging limbs and fallen trees. The horse I was riding insisted upon jumping over every log or mere pole, even those she could easily have just stepped over. Since it was a borrowed horse, I felt no need to hold up the rest of the party trying, in a few minutes, to break the critter of what I considered to be a rather bad habit. Besides, for all I knew, perhaps a previous owner had trained her to jump. So I just sat tight for each jump, and it was not a big deal, —that is, until I miscalculated how high she would leap to very much "over-clear" a small log she could have easily simply stepped over.

The limb, which, with much gusto, knocked my hat off would have cleared a tall rider on an eighteen-hands horse, but not little "Leapin' Leana!" And the pesky limb was not content to roughly knock my shapely hat off. No indeed! It poked a small hole in the crown to boot!

It is true that some horses are spooked by hats, especially large 10-gallon cowboy models. It is also a fact, however, that many horses like hats. More correctly, they enjoy tromping on them or trying to eat them. This can be quite disconcerting if one's head is in the hat at the time!

Yet, another horse on lone was responsible for rather serious damage to my beloved hat, and this without even touching it. This particular steed was one of those show off, "me first" style rascals. Every time I attempted to rein him in to a slower more relaxing pace, so I could enjoy visiting with my fellow riders, he'd "crow-hop" around a bit just to let me know that, if he wanted to, he could show me some real bucking. In spite of this, the short ride went reasonably well until Mr. Fireball (not his real name) sensed that we were heading back to camp. Suddenly, he did a couple more "crow-hops," clenched the bit between his teeth (or so it seemed) and raced full throttle for "home."

There are, of course, some supposedly "safe and sane" (*ha!*) methods for handling such headstrong runaways. If you are certain your reins are good and stout and the bridle is sturdy and secure, you can, hopefully, crank the horse's head around until it is about to touch your knee. Ol' Speedy will most likely stop, or at least just dance around in a tight, slow circle. Of course, there is also the risk that, in utilizing this tactic, your horse might lose his balance and footing and fall down, or worse, somersault. This, in turn, could result in a broken neck to the horse, and possibly the rider as well. Not good! What if you break a rein or slip a bridle in attempting this tight circle method—then what? Just imagine your car is doing about 75 m.p.h., the cruise control is stuck, you have no brakes, and then the steering wheel comes off in your hands! It would be somewhat like that.

If you are certain there are no serious, dangerous obstacles ahead, perhaps it's wise to just put the spurs or whip to Lightning 'til he or she is tuckered out and winded. When the horse finally comes to a belated slow walk, maybe its little horsey brain will forget that it ran away with you. Perhaps it will think, *Mean ol' you—you made me go faster than I wanted to go!* This way the ol' dobbin won't think it got away with something.

But back to my hat—in my runaway, I actually did none of the above. It was not far to camp, and, thankfully, "Fireball" skidded to a stop when he came to the fence.

No cowboy or cowgirl likes to lose a hat for no good reason. It's embarrassing. Mere speed is not a good reason for letting one's hat fly off. Consequently, when "Fireball" took flight, I gave the brim of my hat

No cowboy or cowgirl likes to lose a hat for no good reason. It's embarrassing.

a mighty yank to pull the hat down tight on my head. In so doing, I tore the brim a bit loose from the front of the crown. So you see, it was mostly the fault of the horse that I injured my precious hat. (A little blame is also left over for friend Doug T. for having loaned me his "rocket horse" and especially for laughing about the affair! I should sue him for a new hat!)

A major consolation for my horse-related hat damage is that I was, at least, having fun when it occurred. Much of that which led to its eventual demise, however, was of much more mundane fashion. For instance, working under the hood of a car or under the car itself can inflict considerable damage to a large straw hat. Often, when the hat became more of a hindrance than a help, I would remove it and gently place it in a convenient location. Sometimes that was on the ground. In short, rain, snow, hail, sunshine, sweat, dirt, dust, and grease all took their toll. My poor Durango was not merely bruised and battered it was also filthy dirty.

I decided the least I could do for the poor thing was to give it a sponge bath then apply some globs of lovely white caulking type glue to its various and sundry injuries. I knew the difficult cleaning operation required a powerful cleansing agent. I opted for a nice, semi-clean rag generously soaked with gas.

Alas! Oh, the heartbreak! Woe is me! My battered but still somewhat sturdy and shapely sombrero was almost instantly transformed into a loose, floppy, spineless, but still filthy soft-shell of its formerly handsome self!

Come to think of it—and even though I hate to admit it—my old hat and I have a lot in common. I too have a lot of years and miles on me. Most of us with any years behind us have endured some hard knocks. Life is not all fun and games. My tattle-tale mirror shouts of things I prefer not to think about, much less, acknowledge.

Thankfully, the Holy Bible points us to a major, comforting difference between us and mere things, such as hats: "For which cause we faint not; but though our outward man perish, yet the inward man is renewed day by day. For our light affliction which is but for a moment, worketh for us a far more exceeding and eternal weight of glory" (2 Cor. 4:16–17).

"My Aching Back"

Even though it happened about sixty-six years ago, I still vividly recall exactly where it took place. Little wonder, I guess, since it has had such an adverse effect upon my life, and especially so now that I have attained to "geezerhood." But, I'm way ahead of my story.

In the high mountainous country of North Pine Creek where I was raised, the winters were usually a real challenge, to put it mildly. Perhaps the old timers living there had heard of 4-wheel drive vehicles, but I had not. It's for certain none of the ranchers living in our North Pine Creek, Lemanasky neck of the woods had one. Consequently, with few exceptions, we were not far into winter before our roads became clogged with deep, heavy snow. Our vehicles had to be left down at the bottom of the steep Wingo Hill or at South Pine Creek near the Beeman School. Travel then, which was quite limited, was mostly via skis, snowshoes, horse drawn bobsleds, or horseback.

Incidentally, I fairly well remember the first "snowmobile" (of sorts!) I ever saw. It was built by neighbor kid Bob Smith, who was several years older than I, and, in my eight-year-old opinion, somewhat of a mechanical genius. He cut a nice round section about a foot or so long from a tree trunk, then nailed some strips across it for traction. To one end of it he attached a belt pulley. If I recall correctly he somehow attached it to a couple "arms" and mounted it to the rear of his genuine, store-bought sled. A small Briggs & Stratton gas engine turned the "tree trunk paddle wheel." It actually worked, more or less, on hard packed or frozen snow.

Bob didn't patent his contraption, so a few years later I set out to copy his wondrous machine. I used the gutless gas Maytag motor from Mom's washing machine. Unfortunately, my model was not nearly as well engineered as Bob's, and it was "geared" way too high and had no clutch. It couldn't even take off on level, hard packed snow.

I "wisely" concluded that, if I gave it a good fast start down the smooth, steep hill beside our Jenkins Place house, it would just keep going full speed ahead to Tonasket, a distance of ten miles or so. Kind of like starting a stick shift car downhill in high gear. I could, at least, make it the mile or so to Cook's place where I could show the lovely Cook girls what a sharp guy I was! Sadly, my fine plan only partially succeeded.

I could, at least, make it the mile or so to Cook's place where I could show the lovely Cook girls what a sharp guy I was!

As I picked up more and more speed, it rather belatedly occurred to me that I had no way to stop the motor. Also, the fact that my crude apparatus all clung there at the tail end of my sled, combined with the fact that I was sitting up somewhat, steering with my feet, prevented me from braking in the usual "drag your feet, ruin your overshoes" emergency fashion! Fortunately, the drive belt jumped off my home-made, out-of-round drive pulley, and I slowed to a gentle crawl just before running into the house.

Dad rather urgently "suggested" that it would be best to put my very few inventive talents on hold until I got to be about eighteen, or possibly even twenty-one. At the time, I couldn't figure out whether he was actually worried about my physical well being or merely concerned over the possibility of losing a "hired man" who basically worked just for room and board. By the way, I still have the old Maytag motor—perhaps I should try again!

But—excuse me—I digress. It seems to have become a habit of my age. Mind you, I'm not old; it's just that I was born a long time ago! Now, where were we? Oh, yes, now I remember. My aching back and horse-drawn bobsleds. As they were pulled along, their axles kept the snow shaved off and leveled. Most of our very few neighboring ranchers dragged a heavy, old iron implement wheel behind one of their sled's runners. This made sort of a path for easier walking. I trust that you can now conjure up a mental picture of the procedure.

Now, add to your imagination this fact—when well frozen, the scraped snow became almost as hard as concrete. Once in a while, however, it would warm up, and we would enjoy a brief thaw. Then, all too soon, the thermometer would again drop like the proverbial rock, and the snow "sidewalk" would become still harder. This was the case in "My Aching Back" winter.

That winter younger brother Garry and I had to ride horseback several miles to the Lemanasky Lake schoolhouse. This, of course, included urging our poor horses up the steep Wingo Hill. Getting out of bed early, doing chores, gulping a hasty breakfast, then saddling two horses, and then riding those cold miles to school was a real ordeal. When we, at last, arrived at school, we still had to unsaddle and water and feed our horses at the little schoolhouse barn.

We decided we could save a little time and trouble if we rode double and took just one horse. We disqualified Raven from the task as he could be rather skittish and unpredictable, even though he was faster. Short, stocky little Nippy was, to some degree, Raven's opposite. He was inclined to be a lazy plodder, but he had heart and stamina, and nothing much ever seemed to bother him. We often rode him double even bareback, and he never gave us any trouble.

We certainly were not about to ride those many miles up and down steep hills bareback. As the older brother, I, of course, got to sit on the saddle convincing little bother—excuse me—*brother* that he'd be warmer on the rear "seat" and that he could even take a nap back there if he felt so inclined. All went well on our trip to school that day, but heading home after school was an altogether different story.

As I wrote at the beginning of this story, I still remember almost the exact spot near the top of Wingo Hill where it happened. We had had one of those thaw-freeze weather changes, and my "snow-sidewalk" comparison fit quite well. As I recall, it was so hard that even Nippy could walk on it.

We were just plodding smoothly along, paying no attention to much of anything, much less to Nippy's head or ears when, suddenly, with no warning whatever, he shifted into a bucking mode that we never dreamed he even had in his little computer! Garry just slid rather deftly off over Nippy's bouncing, jerking rump, but I was tossed several feet up into the sky—or so it seemed. When I came down, I landed flat on my back across the edge of that hard concrete "sidewalk." I learned what it is like to "see stars" from pain for a second or two, and then blacked out. When I came to, I feared that I might die before I finally got my breath back. After a while, I somehow struggled painfully back up into the saddle. Nippy acted as though nothing had happened, and we resumed the long ride home.

(Just now as I write, I can't remember if we were ever certain as to exactly why Nippy bucked that day. If I'm not mistaken, that was the only time he ever bucked, at least during the years we owned him. I prefer to believe that brother Garry may have accidentally whacked him with his tin lunch kit or kicked him a little too aggressively in the flanks, but possibly I was to blame. In general practice, we never felt the need for using spurs on our saddle horses. But, as I recall, I had bought a pair mostly so I could at least look the part of a genuine, sure 'nuff rodeo cowboy.)

In those days and with our tough, macho cowboy culture, and with money hard to come by, a few guys might, if "lucky," go to the hospital to die. A few women might even be able to go there to have babies, but, for the most part, we steered clear of doctors and hospitals if we possibly could do so.

Be all that as it may, the upshot is this: off and on for much of my life I have suffered with an aching back. It was a couple of years or so after the "Nippy episode," when it was time for me to register for the draft, that a doctor-ordered x-ray revealed a poorly healed fracture in a major bone the name of which I've forgotten and prefer not to become better acquainted with. Thankfully, for the most part, I have done and am doing quite nicely, and this includes physical activities. I am discovering, however, that when my back goes "out on leave," it takes longer to come back on duty than it did when I was younger.

But now, there are lessons to be learned from all this beside that of paying attention when riding on a horse, yes, even if he or she is a trusted pet and an old nag. I'll wax bold and point out a couple that come readily to mind. You, of course, are welcome to find some of your own.

(a) Some of the things which shape our lives for good or for ill can take place in mere seconds or, at most, in only a few minutes.

(b) Most of us, including this writer, are much like Nippy. We may be moseying smoothly, peaceably down the trail of life when something or someone strikes us wrong, and suddenly we find ourselves in a bucking, fighting mode that we sincerely believed we had deleted from our computer. Volumes beyond number have been written on this topic, this problem. In closing this story, I choose simply to direct our thinking to these few inspired words found in the New Testament book of Hebrews: "Wherefore, seeing we also are compassed about with so great a cloud of witnesses, let us lay aside every weight, and the sin which doth so easily beset us, and let us run with patience the race that is set before us. Looking unto Jesus the author and finisher of our faith; who for the joy that was set before Him endured the cross, despising the shame, and is set down at the right hand of the throne of God" (Heb. 12:1–2).

12.
Exploring

The excitement of the find still stirs me!

For the most part, our lives on the ranch were busy. There always were all manner of chores to attend to. Little brother Garry and I knew better than to ever express boredom, much less use the phrase that was and is commonly used by kids of today and yesterday— "There's nothing to do!" Dad would have speedily found plenty for us to do, most of which would have been a lot less fun than merely being bored!

One of the things we especially enjoyed doing was what we termed "exploring." This simply involved hiking or riding horseback over the hundreds of acres of mountainous, forested land that comprised our cattle ranch and the thousands of acres adjoining it.

The term "riding the range" meant a lot more than rounding up cattle, which was pretty much a seasonal task. Riding the range included counting critters, checking water holes and salt blocks, mending fences, checking the condition of forage, and many other things. What Garry and I particularly liked about it was that Dad could never be for sure whether we were doing the job or merely goofing off! In truth, the task lent itself quite nicely to our love of *exploring*.

We took great pleasure in arriving at some extremely remote spot where we would solemnly declare, "I'll bet no one else has ever been here before." Once in a "blue moon," our bold confidence would be ruined by stumbling across a half buried brown beer bottle or a rusty tin can, probably left by some hunter, cowboy, or Indian some fifty plus years before. Ancient decaying tree stumps left by the logging of many years past sometimes assured us that we were not the first humans to set foot in a particular spot since God created it in the first place. Yep, exploring can be rather disappointing at times.

The old Andy Starr mine was located on land we either owned or leased—I don't remember which. I mostly remember how it intrigued me. The intrigue was enhanced a great deal by the fact that it was rumored to have deep shafts filled to the brim with what appeared to be harmless little pools of water. It also had ladders that looked to be solid and safe but were, in fact, dangerously unstable.

As kids we liked to imagine that perhaps ol' Wilbur who came and worked at the mine a few days each year to keep his claim valid had secretly devised a shortcut to China via some deep secret shaft. After all, he seemed mighty peculiar to us. He was the only adult we had ever seen who would tear up and blubber and bawl over things we didn't even think were sad!

Dad said that we should never explore the Starr mine, but, later on, we kind of "reasoned" that "shouldn't" is not quite the same as "don't," but that's another story.

Sometimes our exploring took us into places so remote and off the beaten path that, had it not been for the Lookout Station perched high atop Aeneas Mountain, we could have become lost. If Mom and Dad asked where we had been I could honestly reply, "I don't know" because, in all probability, we'd be hard pressed to retrace our steps back to wherever we had been.

One memorable day we were *exploring* on the mountain just west of the Jenkins' place where we lived at that time. Actually, as the crow flies, it wasn't all that far from home. However, because of a veritable jungle of trees, thick brush, and boulders, it seemed almost like a far away country.

We fought our slow, tedious way, through the low hanging tree limbs and the scratching, clinging brush, into a small opening of sorts. We could scarcely believe what we saw!

There before us nearly but not quite completely hidden by brush and trees was a wooden door in the mountain. Yes, the wood door was badly decayed, but it was a door, and it was partly ajar. We had chanced upon an ancient, abandoned mine. I still can almost feel a little of the excitement we experienced that day so many years ago.

Fearing that bears or cougars might be holed up in there, we pulled the old door open a little wider as best we could. Then we stood to the side and yelled and threw rocks into the darkness of the tunnel. We were relieved when nothing happened, but we knew we had a problem.

The problem was that we had no kind of light with us, and, worse, we knew that if we told Dad about our wondrous discovery, he would sternly demand, "No exploring, it could be dangerous!" But we did so much want to do so.

A few days later when Dad and Mom had business in town, we obeyed the demands of our urgent curiosity. Armed with a dim and smoky kerosene lantern and my badly worn untrustworthy Winchester .22 rifle (which, incidentally, I still have), we set out to do some mine exploring. Actually it didn't take long.

As I recall, the damp, musty tunnel went pretty much straight back through solid rock a hundred feet or so then made a sharp right turn into a small room of sorts.

I took a quick gasping breath when I saw them standing there in the dim light of the lantern.

I took a quick gasping breath when I saw them standing there in the dim light of the lantern. No, it wasn't old miners—not even their ghosts. It was even better. (Or was it worse?) Picks, shovels, and rock bars stood leaning against the rock wall right where the miners had left them many decades in the past. They were in surprisingly good condition. Evidently the climate in the mine was such that it kept them quite well preserved.

The problem was that they were much too valuable for two frugal ranch kids to leave. If I recall correctly, it took two trips to lug them all home. Their value and usefulness sort of offset Dad's concern for what we had done and what we had discovered. And, after all, he had never told us to stay out of the old Huey Lawrence mine. No one had even thought or known of it for many years. It was only after talking to some "old timers" that Dad found out what it was we had discovered right there on "our" mountain.

Incidentally, in case you are interested, that mountain has been logged and relogged since Garry and I found the mine those many years ago. The opening to the mine has long since caved in and is covered with the growth of trees and brush. The tunnel itself blasted in solid rock might possibly still be there, but I very much doubt if even I could pinpoint the exact location. It has changed too much. But, who knows? If this tired old world continues on long into the future before Jesus returns—which I doubt it will—perhaps some country kid will rediscover the old Hughie Lawrence mine.

In a sense, the exploring we did somewhat reminds me of another type of "exploring"—one with eternal consequence. The careful, diligent study of the Bible, while allowing the Bible's truths to become a part of our lives, can bring treasure that will never lose its value or be lost—not here nor in the better world yet to come.

In Psalm 119, verse 72, King David, in speaking to God, declared, "The law of thy mouth is better unto me than thousands of gold and silver." Hebrews chapter 11 emphasizes the importance of faith in the Christian life. In the last sentence of verse 6, it holds out this challenge and promise: "He that cometh to God must believe that He is, and that He is a rewarder of them that diligently seek Him" (Heb. 11:6). Surely it behooves all of us to do some diligent "exploring" in the Bible, the Word of God.

13.

"Wild Red"

It happened many years ago, and, at the time, I didn't see anything funny about it at all.

Before I had my own auto repair and sales business, I worked as a mechanic at a large automobile agency in Spokane. One day, Jack, one of the used car salesmen, burst into the shop and loudly, laughingly belted out a message on this wise:

"Gentlemen of Hull-Rodell Motors and all inhabitants of Spokane and surrounding areas, I hereby give you fair warning: I just sold a green 1952 Pontiac Sedan to the craziest, wildest driver I've ever had the scariest misfortune of riding with. Indeed, I was afraid I'd not live to give a demonstration drive to another prospect! So, beware of a red-headed gal herding a green 1952 Pontiac two-door sedan."

Knowing Jack, we all just laughed. Hyperbole and dramatics were simply part of his persona. Perhaps that is why "he could sell refrigerators to Eskimos in the dead of winter," as the old line goes.

At that time, my primary work consisted of preparing new cars for delivery, while also working on used cars when their new owners brought them back with various problems they discovered after driving them for a while. The agreed upon proper procedure was for the customer to drive into the main shop service center. The service writer or shop foreman would write up the service order and then bring the car over to the other building where I worked.

My stall was right next to the wide doorway where cars were driven into the building. A short stub wall had been built between the entry way and my stall. This marked off my work area and, likewise, blocked off any wind that chanced to be blowing. It also made my stall appear to be more private and business-like.

The tiny red-headed buyer of the green Pontiac evidently had taken a liking to the dealership and staff and especially to salesman Jack—either that or she simply was bored or lonely with too much time to kill. Because of her too frequent visits, most of us soon learned who she was. There was no mistaking her—she was definitely one of a kind. She was short and tiny, but she made up for that by being loud and sprightly. Perhaps I can best describe her as being *likably obnoxious!* Some of us dubbed her "Wild Red," though never to her face, of course. Yet, thinking back on it, I suspect she'd have been honored had we done so.

But now to the crux of my tale: One memorable day I was lying on my back on my creeper, busily performing major automotive surgery to the underside of an oil dripping car. Suddenly, I heard the distressing roar of an over-revved engine and the squealing of tires on asphalt. These were immediately followed by excruciating pain in my left foot as it was mashed and bent in a direction the Good Lord never intended for it to be bent. To top it off, I reared up and banged my head on the under belly of the car I was working on. As I slid out from under the car, I was in a foggy haze of pain.

My not very sympathetic mechanic buddies later informed me that they had not realized it was possible for a "somewhat normal" person to speedily hop about on one foot while holding the other foot up with one hand while rubbing his head with the other!

By this time, "Wild Red" had leaped from her pampered still-running Pontiac. When I, at last, slowed down a little in my one-foot dance, I began to wager a guess as to what must have happened. "Wild Red" speedily and loudly erased any doubts about what that was.

"I'm sorry! I'm so sorry! Ken, I'm so-o-o sorry I ran over your foot! I'm so-o-o-o VERY SORRY I ran over your foot!"

I appreciated her apology, but it would have seemed considerably more sincere and meaningful had she not been doubled over with gales of laughter as she delivered it.

It happened many years ago, and, at the time, I didn't see anything funny about it. Thankfully, I never suffered any broken bones or permanent damage, however, and I now can see the humor in the affair.

In a rather wry fashion, it kinda reminds me of the way we may, at times, deal with personal sin. 1 John 1:9 in the New Testament promises, "If we confess our sins He [God] is faithful and just to forgive us our sins, and to cleanse us from all unrighteousness." It seems to me we'd better truly mean it when we do so. If we do not, I fear our personal "judgment day" will be no laughing matter. Just something to seriously consider as we near the close of 2014, and, Lord willing, as we experience the "birth" of 2015.

14.
Of Aging and Fire

What a disgusting and disappointing development! I suppose I've looked in the mirror a few million times over these many years, and I never gave it much thought one way or another, that is, until Eleanor and I started looking at some pictures of us taken a few years ago. Big mistake!

I remember looking at thirty- and forty-year-"old" people and thinking, "Boy! —They sure look old!" I determined it would never happen to me. No, I had no intention of dying young. I figured I'd just grit my teeth, set my jaw, scrunch up my body, and make up my mind to just keep looking young. My tattletale mirror screams, "It didn't work!"

Nowadays when kind people say, "Kenny, you haven't changed a bit" I usually reply, "I'm sorry about your eyesight!" If I know them quite well, I jokingly remind them that the Bible warns against "bearing false witness."

I presume the reason becoming "elderly" sneaks up and surprises us is because, for most of us, it does its work so slowly and almost imperceptibly. Although it is speaking of another matter, I am reminded of something the New Testament tells us in James, chapter 1, verses 23 and 24: "If any be a hearer of the word, and not a doer, he is like unto a man beholding his natural face in a glass [a mirror]: For he beholdeth himself and goeth his way, and straightway forgetteth what manner of man he *was*." In other words, it takes a picture of what we looked like years ago to advise us that sneaky old Father Time has been doing a number on us all along.

In my case, however—and possibly yours—it gets worse than simply having our looks go to pot, so to speak.

When I was a child, say about ten to twelve years of age, I somehow jumped to the conclusion that old people knew pretty much everything about everything. It just sort of grew on them. How wrong I was! It now seems the more I know, the more I realize just how little I *do* know. Recently I was honored in being invited to go to a Christian school to (hopefully!) give some tips to grade school kids on storytelling and writing. On the blackboard were some math problems, which I assumed were for a lesson or a test to be given later that day. As I hastily glanced at them, I speedily—and very privately—became painfully aware that, if I had to take the test that day, I would have flunked it for sure. Far from knowing everything about everything now that I have attained "geezerhood," I find I actually know very little, or nothing, about a lot. What a revolting development! It reminds me of something else.

Once again, in keeping with our usual long-standing tradition, I am blessed and relieved to be able to write from my Pine Creek mountain retreat that one of the terrible fires we had here in Eastern Washington came less than two miles from my place. Thanks to God and also some local ranchers and cowboys, my much-cherished hideaway haven was spared.

"FIRE"—now, that's something else I do not truly understand. I looked it up in two old dictionaries. I decided that even Mr. Webster and Mr. or Mrs. Dictionary don't know what fire actually is either. For example, here is one definition: "The visible heat or light produced by burning, a destructive burning, as a forest fire." So I looked up "BURN." "To destroy or damage by fire or heat" Oh! To be sure, some chemist or scientist, and probably some of you, could use some big words such as, FRICTION or CUMBUSTIBLE to describe fire, but I would likely respond with a three-letter word I used quite often as a kid— "WHY?"

Here is how I would use it: *Why* is water so often used to put out fires but when sprayed on certain chemicals it starts a fire? I told you I don't know much. But, that too reminds me of something involving fire—

Younger brother Garry and I conducted an ingenious scientific experiment which resulted in fire. Having run out of ammunition for our BB gun, we became desperate. When we dropped little sticks, twigs, and pebbles down the barrel they often were the wrong size and got stuck. We discovered that wooden matches worked just fine. Moreover, there was an added, exciting bonus. When shot against the side of the hot living room stove, the matchhead exploded with a most delightfully loud "BANG!" along with smoke and a flash of fire.

Sadly, for some strange reason, Mom didn't seem to appreciate our brilliant scientific experimenting, and she rather urgently requested that we conduct it outside—which we did.

We discovered that, when we shot a large rock, the experiment was nearly as successful and satisfying as the hot stove procedure. We also discovered something unexpected. Sometimes there was a "dud" or, at least, a match that pretended to be a "dud." Whenever this happened, we simply reloaded a fresh, new match and moved on in search of another likely looking rock to shoot.

Unfortunately, after we had turned our backs on one of the "duds" and moved away, one of the "duds" came back to life in a lot of highly combustible dry grass and pine needles. I wonder how many other dedicated inventors have peed—or nearly peed their pants—in frantic attempts to correct an experiment gone awry? And all this before their fathers should, perchance, wish to stop their attempts to bless the world by their ingenuity.

(Incidentally, still being of a curious nature, just a few days ago, I got out my Red Ryder BB gun and tried to recapture the thrilling days of childhood. Sadly, it didn't work very well. I suspect these modern safe matches are the reason that nearly every one of them I shot was a slow burning "dud." At least I did not shoot my eye out.)

Yes, fire is a fearful, wondrous thing—whatever it is. Little wonder, I suggest, that God, in the Bible, uses it in many different contexts and for many different purposes. He even uses fire to represent His Holy Spirit, or, at least to represent the work of the Holy Spirit.

No, I don't know all about fire—especially God's fire. And I'm glad I don't. It's satisfying to learn about, although, at times, it is a bit scary.

15.
The Treasure

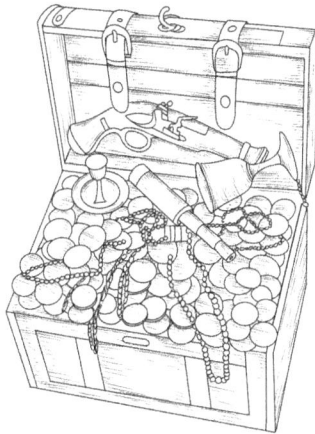

I don't remember if I saw the picture in a geography book or a history book, but, as a nine- or ten-year-old kid, it certainly made an impression on me—and, so much so, in fact, that I'll admit that my imagination may have added some features which were not in the original.

In my mind's eye, I see not only a sturdy expensive looking treasure chest—the contents of which I covet (or at least admire)—containing jewels, diamonds, gold coins, shiny swords and knives, black powder rifles (that, although ancient, still look like new), pistols, and derringers. All such items I was certain I could put to good use, if only I had them.

The gold-plated chest sat next to a deep hole and a large pile of sand. It somewhat disturbed me that I couldn't decide whether the pirates who stood around it were about to bury it or had just dug it up. Since the chest was so clean and solid appearing, it seemed most likely that they were about to bury it. I much preferred the latter. This allowed me to daydream that perhaps when I grew up and knew most everything, I would recognize the spot, dig up the chest, and, at long last, become the rightful owner of all that precious, valuable loot. "Finders keepers, losers weepers!"

It did concern me a little that the pirates looked so tough and mean—especially the one with the black patch over one eye, a wooden peg for his left leg, and a long barreled wicked looking pistol stuck in his belt. I reasoned, however, that maybe he wasn't quite as mean and dangerous as he looked in the picture. He couldn't be all that bad or he wouldn't let that big parrot sit on his shoulder. He probably was the oldest and the boss of the other two pirates.

He looked real old—maybe even as old as thirty-five or forty! Thus, they would probably all be dead by the time I grew up. This cheered me considerably!

It is little wonder, I suppose, that all this gave me the idea for a secret treasure of my own. Obviously I didn't have a nice treasure chest, but it did not take much pawing through the trash to find a good-sized tobacco can with a tight-fitting lid. The difficult part was deciding what to put into it for my buried treasure.

I decided it should be things of value and items that would be useful if I ever got lost or if I ever fell upon hard times sometime way off in the distant future. I hope it will not surprise or disappoint you to hear that, after about seventy-five years, I have forgotten many of the things I chose for my "treasure." I do, however, remember a few of my most "valued" items—

Several 22 cartridges—they evidently dated way back to when my dad was a teenager. They were so old they refused to fire. In fact, I had tried them so many times that the gun's firing pin had misshapen their base as I tried rotating them in the gun's firing chamber. I reasoned that, if the Campbells were starving, I'd dig one up, a miracle would take place, and I would shoot a grouse for emergency sustenance, thereby becoming a hero for the rest of our lives.

I also enclosed a rusty one-bladed pocket knife. Actually, it was about one quarter of a knife blade since most of the blade had been broken off. I couldn't bear to throw it away, so I deemed it to be a "keepsake treasure" and lovingly dropped it into the can.

I deeply regretted my lack of diamonds and gold coins, so, just in case in the future I became desperately poor, I forced myself to put about half my cherished life savings into the treasure can. If I recall correctly, it was the vast sum of one dime and three or four pennies. It was enough that over the years, when I chanced by the special spot where I finally buried my treasure, it gave me a good feeling. It was comforting to know that I wasn't truly "broke" or poor. I had a secret "fortune" stashed away!

When I buried my prized treasure "chest" no more than a half mile from our house at our Jenkins Ranch place, I was careful and cautious. No one but me must know about my treasure, much less, where it was—*or still is.*

So you ask, "Kenny, are you telling us that you never ever dug it up again?" Yep, it's still there—almost certainly—it's still there.

I buried it at the edge of what was then, so many years ago, a plush open meadow. Over these many years it has become a lush grove with a lot of thick, clinging brush. The large rock I rolled on top of it for a marker has been rolled over many times by bears who turn over rocks to find food—ants and beetles that make their homes under the rocks. There are dozens of similar looking rocks scattered here and there over those acres of trees and thick brush.

The truth of the matter is that I simply "outgrew" my treasure. Oh, to be sure, I still get a kick out of those rare occasions when I chance to drive by that memorable spot. I may even tell any passengers this story, but I very much doubt whether I could find my "treasure" even if I wanted to.

I guess it boils down to this—we can never be truly "broke" so long as we have pleasant, warm memories. I hope you have experienced, as Eleanor and I have, that most of our fondest memories involve friends and loved ones—but especially God and His leading.

Speaking of God—do you suppose *He* has treasure? "Possibly," you reply, "but why would He?" Does not the Bible tell us, "He owns the cattle on a thousand hills." (Raised on a cattle ranch as I was that's impressive!) And does not the Bible's book of Revelation speak of God's heaven containing all manner of precious stones including gold? Yes, definitely.

Just as definitely God has and cherishes His treasure. It is more valuable and precious to Him than this old world or anything in it, with one major exception, which we discover in the last book of the Old Testament, Malachi. Here it is:

> Then they that feared [loved] the LORD spake often one to another: and the LORD hearkened, and heard it, and a book of remembrance was written before Him for them that feared [loved] the LORD, and that thought upon his name. And they shall be mine, saith the LORD of hosts, in that day when I make up my jewels; and I will spare them, as a man spareth his own son that serveth him. (Mal. 3:16–17)

Yes, I pretty much "outgrew" my "treasure," but God will never outgrow His treasure. He wants *you*—He wants us—to be His *treasure* for eternity. The choice is ours, you know. The "whosoever" of John 3:16 is for anyone and everyone!

16.
High-Speed Cultivating

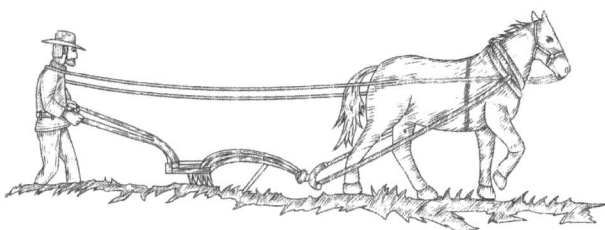

From out of the south came the thundering hoof beats of the *great horse*. Nah!—it wasn't Silver and the Lone Ranger, and, to be truthful, the horse involved, as you shall learn, wasn't so great either. But it is a great line! I've always wanted to pilfer it, and—besides—it does kind of fit. So there!

This all-too-true story begins with our large potato patch located about a quarter mile southeast of our house at Lemanasky Lake. It seems that a lot of naughty bad weeds were attempting to strangle most of the potato plants. Potatoes were much needed for the sustenance of the Campbell family. Therefore, dear old Dad determined that he must speedily come to their rescue. In fact, Dad's motto seemed to be, "Anything worth doing is worth doing right, and that speedily!"

At breakfast one fine summer morning, Dad announced that he intended to cultivate the entire several acre potato patch that day. He mused that good old, dependable horse Topsy was getting too slow, and, since his brush with death (and that's "material" for another story), little Franky had calmed down considerably and could easily pull the small cultivator in fine fashion. He would do so in about half the time it would take old Topsy to plod slowly along up and down between row after long row of potato vines.

After breakfast, Dad harnessed Franky with no problems and happily headed down the road for the potato patch. He had hauled the cultivator there in the pickup the preceding day.

None of us were there to witness and learn the fine points of "high speed cultivating." It's easy to visualize, however, if you have any knowledge of old one-horse cultivators. Likewise, it is easy to explain—even if you are too young or "cityfied" to be knowledgeable of such old-fashioned matters.

One-horse cultivators have two handles similar to a musher's sled that is pulled by dogs. The horse—Franky, in this case—is hitched to the cultivator. Long leather "lines" are fastened to the bridle bit in the horse's mouth. In the case of a saddle horse, shorter "lines" are called "reins." In car terms, maybe we can liken the lines to the steering wheel and, hopefully, functioning brakes besides.

OK, so now you've got the picture. However, Dad had a not-so-slight problem that day. You see, Franky was not trained in the fine art of staying in the "center lane" between the rows of potato vines. Straying even a little too far right or left will obviously result in pulling up the precious plants. Franky needed frequent tugs on the lines to keep him in the straight and narrow, but constantly holding both the cultivator handles and the lines is nigh on too impossible.

Dad's usual solution was quite simple. He tied the ends of the lines together, thus making a "loop" which he then put over his head and down across his back. To prevent the loop from falling down further, one side of the "loop" went under one arm, and the other side went over the opposite shoulder. Great! The lines were now near at hand without needing to be constantly held. The skilled cultivator operator—in this case Dad—could now concentrate on trying, in some small degree, to steer the cultivator, developing blisters on his hands, and hitting an occasional buried rock, which caused the cultivator handle to whack his ribs. Then, from time to time, he could let go of one of the handles for a second or two—just long enough to give a hasty pull on Franky's "steering wheel."

So, Franky and Dad are cultivating at a nice pace. Dad is thinking: *This job will be done in half the time it would take with ol' Topsy.* Then the unexpected happens—a large grouse, in a flurry of feathers and loudly drumming wings, takes flight practically under Franky's nose. He is spooked and his reflexes are excellent.

Then the unexpected happens—a large grouse, in a flurry of feathers and loudly drumming wings, takes flight practically under Franky's nose.

He speed shifts through second and third gears, then hits high gear in about four seconds flat. In about an equal amount of time Dad is mostly "air borne." According to his later account, his feet only hit the high spots now and then. Weeds and potato vines are being launched into space from both sides of the cultivator. And, mind you, this was long before the means to travel into "space" had even been invented! Dad is afraid to let go of the cultivator handles because he probably will lose his balance and momentum just long enough to knock all his teeth out on the iron crossbar of the cultivator.

To further complicate his predicament, remember that the lines are knotted behind his back! They basically have him tied to the source of the problem—Franky! In Franky's fright, with the cultivator banging his rear end every few feet and evidently forgetting his limited knowledge of human vocabulary, he thinks the loudly screamed command, "WHOA! WHOA!" means, *FASTER! FASTER!*

Dad clings to one desperate hope of "release" and "salvation." He is thinking: *At this speed, we'll reach the fence in just a few more seconds and Franky will have to stop!* Remember Dad's motto? "Anything worth doing is worth doing right!" Dad sometimes, rather tongue-in-cheek, boasted, "My fences would hold an elephant!" Too bad Franky didn't know that!

With the screeching of barbed wire and the loud splintering of fence posts, Franky plunged right through the fence and sped full throttle up the road in the direction of home. Somehow, in going through the fence, Dad and the remains of his twisted cultivator were miraculously released from Franky.

I was at the well alongside the road when, out of the south, came the thundering hoofbeats of the not-so-great horse Franky! He looked neither right nor left, and, without slowing down even a little bit, bolted around the corner by the old Didra log barn and vanished in a cloud of dust.

In times past, in various stories or sermons, I have declared that I never saw my Dad run. I now remember that I have been mistaken. There was one exception—only a minute (or maybe four) after Franky sped past, Dad sprinted into view looking rather like a tattered, torn, somewhat bloody, and very irate scarecrow.

In my surprise and shock, I blurted out one of my stupidest questions ever: "Hey, Dad, did ya have a runaway?" As I recall, Dad yelled something about he and Franky just being out for a little exercise, then sternly commanded, "Jump in the pickup!" Evidently Dad knew Franky would just keep going past home.

The '36 Chevy probably broke a Pine Creek speed record past the schoolhouse, and Dad let 'er "plummet" right on down the steep Wingo Hill.

We found Franky with most—but not all—of the harness, all tangled up and caught in chokecherry bushes at the bottom of the hill. It didn't take Dad long to untangle the panting, trembling little rascal. He snapped a lead rope onto Franky's halter, then tied the other end to one of the chains on the tailgate of the pickup. Franky, no doubt, made the trip back up the hill at about the same speed that he had gone down it!

To our knowledge, Franky never worked as a cultivator puller again. Dad swore he'd had enough "high speed cultivating" to last the rest of his life, and ol' Topsy got her job back. She also got another job as well. After that, Dad always "teamed" Franky up with Topsy.

To be sure, they made a strange looking pair. Some of the neighbors even kidded Dad a little about his team—big, black, steady, plodding, dependable Topsy, and little blue, "Roman-nosed" skittish, young but willing and eager to pull his share of the load and more Franky! What a pair!

Could there possibly be a lesson there for us? I think so. Also—and at the risk of sounding "preachy"—Dad being "tied" to Franky and the cultivator reminds me of something Saint Paul said in regard to being "tied" to our sin-prone human nature. He wrote: "O wretched man that I am! Who shall deliver me from the body of this death?" He then went on to answer his own question (and ours as well) with these words: "I thank God through Jesus Christ our Lord" (Rom. 7:24–25, in part).

I don't know about you, but that sure sounds a lot better to me than being "released" and "saved" by being dragged through a barbed wire fence!

17.
Picking Tomatoes

In view of the stories many of you have heard me tell or that you have read in my book, *Stories I Lived*, you may have gotten the impression that I have always been a hillbilly cowboy kind of guy. I don't know whether to apologize or boast as I inform you that this is not the case.

I was actually born in a hospital in San Jose, California. Granted, in view of my "vintage," said medical facility may have been of rustic construction, somewhat akin to a log cabin. In any event, I suffered considerable slight and embarrassment over the course of many troubling years. This was because I had no birth certificate. In other words, I could not prove that I had even been born, much less that I was not simply homemade!

If I recall correctly—and I have on a few rare occasions been known to recall incorrectly—the problem had something to do with my dear Osage great-grandmother. The story goes that she was so pleased and excited when she saw me, a homely but happy, cooing baby, that she made some kind of smoke signal "typo" to announce my arrival and that in a genuine hospital. Thus, the rest of my tribe became confused as to the actual day and time of my birth. I had to tell you all this so you can better understand and appreciate my story.

In short, my parents took me after my birth to our home in Sunnyvale. There they proceeded to raise me as a somewhat normal city kid for the first seven years of my life. In truth, I was well "cityfied" and dull. I knew nothing about the origins of vegetables, milk, or much else of our farm grown diet. I simply supposed—if I thought about it at all—that the people at the store just made such things themselves.

So, it came to pass that one day long ago Mom asked, "Kenny, would you like to go pick tomatoes with me and the neighbor lady?" Actually, looking back at it now, I suspect it was kind of a bribe. Posing the exciting question several days prior to the eagerly anticipated wondrous event, every now and then she would subtly "remind" me that, *if* I were a "good boy," I could go pick tomatoes. In truth, I had no idea if they grew on trees, underground, or wherever, but it sounded like something I would just love to do. So, take my word for it, I was a very good boy—mostly.

Every morning and several times per day I asked, "Is this the day we go pick tomatoes?" It seemed like eternity, but, at long last, the day arrived—along with the neighbor lady. She and Mom sat at the breakfast table and gabbed and gabbed and visited and laughed 'til I feared I would die of impatience long before we would leave to go pick tomatoes.

When we finally got in the car and headed to wherever the tomatoes were anxiously waiting for me to pick them, it seemed that Mom drove way too slowly. It got better, however, when we had inched out of town. I began to see animals I'd mostly only seen in picture books. These were rare exotic animals such as horses and cows and chickens and pigs and goats and sheep. Oh, I had been to the zoo to see tigers, lions, and elephants. I'd even been scared by monkeys who had shrieked and thrown fecal stuff at us. Mom and Dad later delighted in telling anyone and everyone who would listen that, at the zoo, "Kenny mostly ran up and down on the sidewalk in front of the animal cages excitedly yelling, 'birdy, birdy,' and pointing at the common, plentiful pigeons, seagulls, and sparrows."

I don't remember that, but I do vividly remember the tomato picking trip.

I remember the sunshine and the unusual odors. Some were pleasant, some not at all pleasant. Yes, I remember the birds, the butterflies, the horses, and the cows. But mostly I remember the excitement and happiness of getting to go somewhere I had never been before to do something I had never done before. I remember thinking this is the best day I've ever lived. And I remember how it ended!

So, at long last we drove into the farmyard and down past long rows of green vines with big red tomatoes hanging on them.

Mom had given me my very own little bucket. It didn't take long to fill it. Soon I was eating a very special looking tomato. I didn't care in the least that the juice ran all over my face, then on down my chin and neck, and then on down my shirt and pants. Mom didn't care or even notice. She and the neighbor lady were having such a grand time visiting and laughing and picking tomatoes.

I picked and ate tomatoes for a long time—probably about five minutes. Then I decided I should not waste such a glorious day just picking tomatoes. Over there a block or so away I spied a long, low white building. Curiosity demanded that I go over and check it out.

When I reached the building, I was pleased to see that it had a nice wide full-length sidewalk along one side. It was the ideal size for a "betwixt and between" kid to skip back and forth on. As I did so, I thought on this wise: *What a great day! Even when I'm all growed up I'll want to do this!* After all, I was "betwixt and between"—about four or five years of age.

On one of my joyous trips back and forth on the wide sidewalk, I noticed something very interesting. One end of the sidewalk was at about ground level, but the other end was higher—probably about four feet higher. What interested me most, however, was a large pile of brownish-greenish something or other. Someone had evidently heaped it up down there.

As I stood there carefully scanning it I thought: *It looks soft!* Hot on the heels of that intriguing thought sprang forth a most daring idea: *I'll bet I could jump in it, and I wouldn't even get hurt!* I, of course, had never heard of the *Guinness Book of Records*, but I cheerfully thought on this wise, *If I jump it might be the biggest and best jump a kid my size and age has ever made.* Mom will be so proud to hear of my bravery!

> *What interested me most, however, was a large pile of brownish-greenish something or other.*

There was, however, one particular challenge. The center of the mound was several feet away from the "launching pad." If I merely just sort of dribbled off the edge of the sidewalk, I'd land in a shallow part of the mound and probably get hurt. I had to be certain I would be well cushioned where I landed.

No real problem—I'd just get up a good bit of speed as I jumped. And that is just what I did. I powered full throttle down the straight-away and sailed somewhat like a large, graceful bird through space. My calculation was excellent. I was right on target. I made a bullseye. (In view of what happened perhaps "bullseye" is an accurate term.)

To my extreme alarm I discovered that my theory regarding the softness of the stinking material into which I had so deftly plunged was, indeed, quite *soft*. So *soft*, in fact, that I sunk down to the upper portion of my chest. Much closer to my sensitive nose than I would have preferred.

This, however, was by no means the worst of my rather delicate situation. I was soundly—or not so soundly—*stuck!* Moreover, when I attempted to put my legs into gear to walk out, I began to sink down still deeper. My joy in picking tomatoes was speedily leaving me—and *not* "high and dry," as the old saying goes.

All this, of course, was while Mom and the neighbor lady were enjoying a pleasant day picking tomatoes and visiting. They were paying no attention to me and my exploring. I had, at first, been glad for that, but not anymore. I pulled my arms and hands up out of the vile manure pile, 'cause that's what I belatedly learned it was, and, with them dripping stinking and slimy stuff, I waved at mom and loudly and frantically yelled, "*Help, Mom!* I'm stuck!"

She quickly looked up, but it seemed to me that her response was not as hasty as my dire predicament deserved. I wondered: *Was she perhaps pondering a weighty decision such as, "Is that dumb kid really worth it?"*

Also, why is the neighbor lady laughing so hysterically while Mom is not laughing at all? Indeed, she looks rather solemn and stern.

Perhaps I should inform you that my mom was rather "vertically challenged," being only about 5'2" or 5'4" tall. Yes, and she wore a lady-like dress even while picking tomatoes. She had to hold up her skirt as she waded ankle deep out to effect the "rescue." I guess we could call it a rescue. She grabbed my slick hand painfully tight and then dragged me quite unsympathetically through the brownish-greenish goo to dry land.

As soon as I felt my feet touch solid ground, I very contritely and politely apologized for soiling my shirt and trousers with tomato juice. Mom did not seem much impressed by my meek, sincere apology. She appeared to have other things on her mind. Perhaps the neighbor lady's loud laughter upset her. It didn't do anything for me either.

As luck would have it, there was a faucet with a hose there at the corner of the barn. (Yes, that's what it was.) Mom turned it on full blast and hosed me down—kinda like you hose off your car. Not content with that, she yanked my shirt off and hosed me down some more. I'll spare *you* the embarrassing details. Suffice it to say that, after each of the five or six items that had hidden my skinny form came off, I felt the full-force blast of the cold-water cleansing until I stood there shivering in my nothingness. My love for picking tomatoes speedily washed down the drain. All this, mind you, while the neighbor lady laughed hysterically.

Mom laughed too—about ten years later. Miraculously, I still like to eat tomatoes, although sometimes I imagine they have a rather pungent odor about them.

Now for a somewhat "preachy" PS: Although this is the first time I have written this story, I've told it now and then to a "select" audience. Not long ago, a lady I had not seen for many years—indeed, I had forgotten her—came up to me and asked, "Have you picked any tomatoes recently?" Kids especially like it for some reason. If I ask for requests of stories they have heard before, some kid is certain to "demand" the tomato picking story.

I get a kick out of asking them if they think my mom should have punished me. The majority usually say "no" for various reasons. "You were just a dumb innocent kid who didn't know better." Or, they say, the stinky ordeal and the harsh water cleaning was sufficient punishment itself. Once a wise little girl solemnly declared, "Your mom should have been punished for not keeping her eye on you!" I liked that one!

When I have asked them if they thought I should be punished if I came back and did it again as a ten- or eleven-year-old, or even as a teenager, they shout an emphatic, *"Yeah!"* So my next question is: "How many of you know right from wrong?" Most hands quickly shoot up, so I drive the lesson home. Come to think of it, the lesson is not just for *kids*.

"The wages of sin is death" (Rom. 6:23). So stay away from Satan's manure pile! Thankfully, "If we confess our sins [and turn from them] *he* [God] will forgive our sins and cleanse us from all unrighteousness" (1 John 1:9)—not with a garden hose, but with the precious blood—and life—of Jesus Christ (1 John 1:19).

18.
Torture Chamber

(That title may be a mite exaggerated, but it is so close to the truth that I thought of it a short time ago when I had a tooth cavity filled and then a haircut on the same day.)

Oh, yeah—I remember it all too well! It usually began when I noticed Dad staring intently at me as we ate breakfast. His steady gaze caused me to search my conscience for some recent naughtiness. I didn't dare go back too far in my memory bank lest I actually remember something. When Dad, at last, said, "Kenny, you're starting to look like a shaggy sheep dog," I feared I was in for it, the much-to-be-dreaded "doomsday" had arrived.

I had gritted my teeth and set my jaw in a very stern fashion in the vain hope that my hair would stop growing, but it had paid me no attention. Not content to merely cover my eyebrows, it had now moved on down with the intent of covering my eyes. I kind of liked the way my hair tried to hide my large protruding ears, but even I did not appreciate what might be considered a rather feminine appearance. Back then, that look would never do. I much preferred the then popular macho cowboy look. While I was not certain that I liked Dad's "shaggy sheep dog" description, I was forced to admit that I could see why he came up with it. There was, indeed, some comparison.

Then, when Dad said, "Right after breakfast go out to the shop and get that old, wooden apple box," there was now no doubt about it—this was the dreaded haircut day!

Now, perhaps you are thinking on this wise: What's so bad about getting a haircut? And why have you compared it to a *torture chamber*? I hasten to explain: We didn't have electricity, and Dad's equipment for the fear-

Dad was meticulous when it came to his axes, saws, and chisels, but, as I understand it, there was no way to sharpen the hair clippers. So, they didn't cut hair; they simply yanked it out by the roots!

some task was a long fine-toothed comb, reserved only for haircutting, which, with its close together teeth, was diabolically designed to pull kid's hair—especially if it chanced to be slightly matted as mine often-times was. (And especially on haircut day!) And what about the hand activated clippers? Perhaps I can best describe them by comparing them to the cruel, wicked instrument we sometimes had to use when dehorning cattle. (If you've never witnessed that procedure, consider yourself lucky.)

Dad was meticulous when it came to his axes, saws, and chisels, but, as I understand it, there was no way to sharpen the hair clippers. So, they didn't cut hair; they simply yanked it out by the roots! Are you beginning to get the picture?

So, there I was, perched precariously up on the shaky up-ended apple box with the stern command to, "Sit still!" In my younger years, to attain a convenient height for barber Dad I had to do this while also sitting upon a thick "Sears and Sawbuck" or "Monkey Wards" catalog. I had a large white sheet—no doubt made from a flour sack—pinned snuggly—no, *tightly* around my neck. Supposedly this was to keep loose hairs from falling down my neck and causing me to itch. It only halfway succeeded, but it did prevent me from natural, normal breathing. Moreover, this device prevented me from engaging in any sissy-type scream of pain. (Can *you* swallow without your "Adam's apple" moving up and down? Try it sometime.)

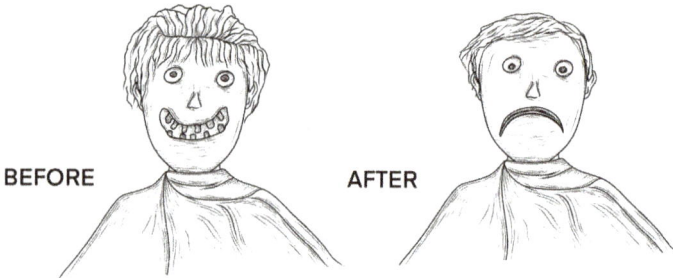

BEFORE   AFTER

Since my arms and hands were, likewise, wrapped firmly under the tight sheet, I may as well have been wearing a straitjacket. Thinking back on it just now, it occurs to me that this may have been Dad's intention. The tight sheet kept me from instinctively grabbing for his hand as the dull clippers yanked a few strands of my precious, solidly affixed hair out by its roots.

Needless to say, even one loose, unattached hair waving freely about on or near one's nose can cause considerable itching. When this happened—and it always did—I would frantically try to blow it off. Mind you, this wondrous feat had to be accomplished without moving my head even as little as a tiny fraction of an inch lest Dad should apply his free hand to my head while sternly admonishing me, "Stop your fidgeting!"

Now, I trust you are not eating and have a "strong" stomach as I lead you through this memorable relating of all too true events of my days of yore. Honesty, however, constrains me to inform you of one particular haircut that was cut somewhat short. I don't simply mean my hair was cut short—it usually was. I mean the *time* devoted to that particular haircut was cut amazingly and abruptly short.

It seems that I was either coming down with or coming out of a bad cold. When I felt a strong sneeze coming on, I tried mightily to suppress it, thus building up considerable pressure. When, at last, the powerful sneeze could no longer be squelched or contained, it *erupted*. Had I been older or more "cultured" or refined, I presume that that which blasted forth from my dripping nostrils would have been mere mucus. *But* ... since I was only about ten years old and far from "cultured," refined, or sophisticated, I must inform you that my face was generously slathered with what it actually was—*snot* and *boogers!*

When it came to macho-type things such as angry people, mean dangerous bulls, kicking cows and horses, Dad was pretty much fearless. But ... that memorable haircut ended when macho ol' Dad gaggingly croaked, "*Vi!* Come here and wipe off your kid's face!" Hastily he released me from the "straight jacket," duck tails, rooster tails, and cowlicks intact—and with that he stomped out into the blessed relief of a blinding minus ten-degree snowstorm.

Now, to you, loyal fans of my annual story-letter (both of you), I know that you have come to expect a bit of sermonizing. Granted, it is a mite challenging after "the above," but, painful as my childhood haircuts were, they cannot in any wise be compared to that which Jesus Christ suffered for you and for me. My haircuts came *far short!* All four gospels—Matthew, Mark, Luke, and John—tell the story. Matthew chapter 27 is particularly detailed and heart wrenching. Quite honestly, I cannot understand how any honest, caring person can read, contemplate, and meditate on that graphic and touching depiction of what Jesus went through for us without being amazed, baffled, and, yes, *changed* by such incredible self-sacrificing love. I strongly urge everyone to read and reread that chapter over again and again in this new year.

19.

A Lesson in Perseverance

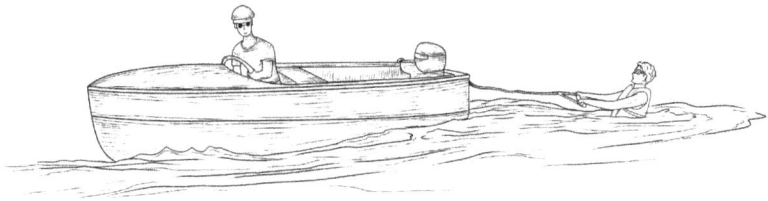

It happened some sixty-five years ago, but in my "mind's eye" I can still see Jim's black hair waving in the breeze just barely above the surface of Hayden Lake. Talk about a lesson in determination, steadfastness, and endurance! But I'm way ahead of the story.

Even though the sport of water skiing was not entirely new in this story that took place many years ago, I believe I am safe in suggesting that it was generally looked upon as being somewhat of a dare-devil activity. At least more than it is now.

It seems that my friend Loren had acquired a "new" used boat. He was eager to see if it was fast enough and powerful enough to pull a water skier. As I recall, there were about four of us young married couples who met at Hayden Lake in Idaho for the exciting, new-to-us adventure.

The ladies *wisely* elected to simply observe for a while—probably to see if any serious injuries or drownings should be involved. So, I was rather sternly urged to "volunteer" to be the first to be trolled behind Loren's boat with clumsy, pointy boards loosely attached to my trembling feet. The "reasoning" resorted to by my "unselfish" friends for urging me to "volunteer" to be first was that, of the men, I was the lightest. I would have been honored had they not gone on to imply that I was the lightest only because of my lack of brains to weigh me down.

Well, to some small degree I lucked out. It was only beginner's luck that I popped right up out of the water on my first attempt. Lurching to the right, and then to the left, and then forward and backward I barely managed to stay mostly on top of the boards I was precariously, shakily standing upon. After a few hundred yards of this torture, Loren took pity upon me and circled back somewhat near where I had taken off.

I would like to inform y'all that I smoothly, gracefully glided into shallow water where I then casually stepped off the skis and onto the blessed, firm, dry land. Unfortunately, it wasn't quite that way. In fact, when I let go of the tow rope, I did that which I suppose could best be described as a spectacular bellyflop, immediately followed by a partially underwater somersault of sorts. I came up spouting water out of my nose, mouth, ears, and anywhere else a somewhat human body can forcefully eject water.

You may correctly conclude that the cheers and applause, which I had felt I so richly deserved by my amazing first time in "getting up," were speedily eradicated and forgotten by the loud, totally unrestrained gales of laughter that fell upon the ears of anyone within a mile or so. It was most humbling.

Now, if you are looking for a hero in this true tale, it quite obviously is not me. As I proceed, however, you, with me, may decide that my long-time buddy, Jim Homburg, comes the closest. In truth, his actions that day so long ago are the reason I've chosen to cite it as an example for us to "hang on" when we are going through the tough, difficult times of our lives.

This said, I shall now describe to you what Jim did on that memorable day so long ago. First of all, however, I must advise you that, in his youth, Jim was very athletic. In fact, as a student at North Central High School in Spokane, he set a high mark in pole vaulting, which stood for a number of years. Also, he is one of only two guys I have seen in my entire life who could firmly grip a flagpole and not merely shinny up it (even I could do that) and somehow "power" his body out to where it was sticking out horizontal from the flagpole, not vertical with it! (He has a picture of him doing this as proof.)

All this would lead one to believe that he would easily and speedily pop up like a professional in his first time on water skis. Alas, it was not to be. Try as he could, he would "wash out" in various hilarious positions of "wipe-outs." His skis would, of course, speedily float away with each and every failed attempt, thus causing him to flounder about in strenuous efforts to retrieve them. Yes, and then he had to put them back on while bobbing and twisting and taking on much water.

As you may well imagine, all this afforded fabulous entertainment for us landlubbers. We stood on the nice warm beach and loudly "cheered him on." We called out encouraging words like, "Keep your skis closer together!" "Don't pull on the rope like that—just let the boat pull you up." "You're leaning too far forward." "You're leaning too far backward!" "Put your rump down deeper in the water." "Don't try to stand up on the skis so quickly!" "You look like a stork tryin' to put on stilts!"

Me being the "expert" (ex-spurt), I shouted the loudest: "Hey, Homburg, if I did it, you can too," followed by, "And if even I can do it anybody can do it—why can't you?!"

By Jim's red face and the hard, icy glares he shot back at us, we could tell he was studiously pondering our wise suggestions. We could also tell that, thanks to us, he was getting better. We had to admit it. Now our most used and truthful encouragement changed to, "You almost made it!" "You let loose of the towrope just as you were coming up!" "You almost had it!" This went on for many more futile attempts before the seeming miracle we witnessed that day occurred. I can still see it in my memory bank.

By this time, I suspect "Captain" Loren may have been a mite tired if, indeed, not somewhat irked over burning so much outboard motor gas and oil for nothing. With Jim at long last back in starting position again and yelling, "*Hit it!*" Loren *hit it. Boy!* did he really *hit it!* There was considerable slack in the towrope—enough that we feared the rope handle would be snatched out of Jim's hands, or, much worse, his arms would be jerked off. Fortunately, neither happened. Jim held on, and *boy! did he ever hang on!*

With all this build-up to the story, you surely and logically would expect me to inform you that Jim popped up on the surface of the water and took off like an old pro. *Not so*—what would be the miracle in *that?* Jim did NOT "come up," in fact, impossible as it may seem, he sank down deeper into the water! At that time, he sported a full, generous head-full of dark, almost black wavy hair. That and his hands firmly, stubbornly, tenaciously gripping the towrope handle were about all we could see as he and the boat headed out to sea.

Try to imagine a submerged submarine with only its periscope showing above the surface of the water, and the periscope is wearing a dark wavy wig as it plows through the water at a lively pace pushing a considerable wake. OK—now you have a general idea of the picture that still shines clearly in my memory bank.

I have no idea what the skis were doing down deep under Jim, if indeed, they were still there. And how could Jim hold his breath *so long*? And is it possible to drown while standing up—is he even standing up—since all we could see was the top of his head with his hair frantically waving in the breeze?

We only know this was the "miracle" we saw that day. It continued until they, at last, disappeared from our view as they went around a bend in the shoreline.

I will conclude this account by telling you that when they came back, Jim was in the boat with Loren. We gave him a rather joyous—in fact—laughing ovation for *hanging on* and not giving up. (Later that same day, he *did* get up on the skis, and he skied as well or better than I had.)

As I have struggled over how to share a little of what this year has brought by way of challenge to Eleanor and myself—and probably to many of you—I could not think of a better example of "*hanging on*" and not giving up than I have just shared.

Thanks, Jim. I trust this will not embarrass you. But, come to think of it, your dear friends deserve much of the credit for your hanging on for so-o-o-o lo-o-o-o-ng. You probably would not have performed such a wondrous feat had we not so thoughtfully and vociferously *jeered* you on!

My Austin's Amazing Homecoming

Cars have been my hobby and business for practically all my life. It's a fact that I like old cars both large and small. To say that I love one more than another would be somewhat like asking a set of parents which one of their kids they like best.

That being said, I will admit that my crush on the American Austin began nearly seventy-five years ago when I was nine years old. An acquaintance of my parents drove up in a cute, little car, which I judged to be about my size. It was an American Austin. The owner's name was Mr. Carr, and I determined, right then and there that, when I "got big," I would have one.

It took about eighteen years. In 1957, I realized my dream and acquired one. It was fairly rough, had a major driveline problem, but I was happy to have it sitting in my yard. Sadly, I was too busy with other more important matters and never had time to play with it. When a friend offered to trade me for a badly needed garage, I made the swap and fought back tears as he hauled it away.

Over the next fifty-five years or so, I thought about my little Austin and wondered what had become of it and if it even still existed. My friend had sold it not long after getting it from me. During those years, I started my own auto repair business and became a licensed, bonded auto dealer for thirty years. It was somewhat natural to find myself the owner of many collector type vehicles. They only slightly dulled the ache whenever I thought of my lost Austin.

Then in March of 2015, some friends from out of town came over to visit, and we helped them look for a nice preowned RV. Having been a dealer for so long, I knew my way around Spokane, so we took them to a few dealerships. I remembered that a fellow dealer was associated with one of the car lots years ago. Mind you, we had only done business a few times at least twenty years before and were never what you called close friends. We just knew each other from both being dealers.

Well, I asked the salesman if "Monte" was still in the country or if he had ever heard of him. "Indeed he is," was the reply. "In fact, he owns this dealership."

Impulsively, I said that he might remember me, and I handed the salesman one of my radio cards. (At that time, I hosted a Christian radio broadcast.)

Monte called me that very evening, and he told me breathlessly, "Ken, you're not going to believe this, but today I bought an American Austin from a lady in Edwall, Washington. I found an old registration in it in your name. Could it have been your car?"

A few days later we made the deal. I hated to say goodbye to a Nash Metropolitan in trade, but it felt great to realize that my cherished little Austin had come home after nearly sixty years. By the way, it still had the same problems that it had those many years ago. And it looks about the same as well. When I bid it a fond farewell so long ago, I took a picture on that day, and it's been on my bulletin board all these years.

I've worked on it off and on over the last few weeks. Now that I have "gotten big" (as I had described when I was nine) as well as old, it gives me much pleasure to herd it slowly around under its own power. To be sure, my wife, Eleanor, thinks I have too many cars. It's difficult to argue otherwise with her. But the Austin that came home after nearly sixty years is an altogether different story.

It just seems it was meant to be!

So, my little American Austin had a truly amazing homecoming, but I am eagerly looking forward to a much better homecoming, one of *eternal* consequence. So, to conclude this book, I'll allow Jesus Christ to tell of it in His own words:

"In my Father's house are many mansions; if it were not so, I would have told you, I go to prepare a place for you. And if I go and prepare a place for you, I will come again, and receive you unto myself, that where I am there you may be also" (John 14:2–3).

Let us personally determine to be a part of *that*—the *greatest story of all!*

AMEN.

Kenny

TEACH Services, Inc.

P U B L I S H I N G

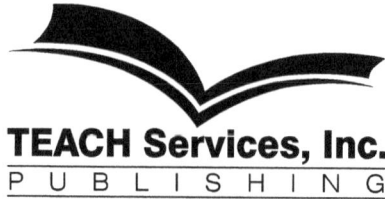

We invite you to view the complete
selection of titles we publish at:
www.TEACHServices.com

We encourage you to write us
with your thoughts about this,
or any other book we publish at:
info@TEACHServices.com

TEACH Services' titles may be purchased in
bulk quantities for educational, fund-raising,
business, or promotional use.
bulksales@TEACHServices.com

Finally, if you are interested in seeing
your own book in print, please contact us at:
publishing@TEACHServices.com

We are happy to review your manuscript at no charge.

www.ingramcontent.com/pod-product-compliance
Lightning Source LLC
Chambersburg PA
CBHW060553100426
42742CB00013B/2537